THE 100 MOST DIFFICULT BUSINESS LETTERS YOU'LL EVER HAVE TO WRITE, FAX, OR E-MAIL

THE 100 MOST DIFFICULT BUSINESS LETTERS YOU'LL EVER HAVE TO WRITE, FAX, OR E-MAIL

Clear Guidance on How to Write Your Way Out of the Toughest Business Problems You Will Ever Face

BERNARD HELLER

HarperBusiness
A Division of HarperCollins*Publishers*

HarperCollins books may be purchased for educational, business, or sales promotional use. For information please write: Special Markets Department, HarperCollins Publishers, Inc., 10 East 53rd Street, New York, NY 10022.

FIRST EDITION

Designed by Irving Perkins Associates

Library of Congress Cataloging-in-Publication Data

Heller, Bernard.
   The 100 most difficult business letters you'll ever have to write, fax, or e-mail : clear guidance on how to write your way out of the toughest business problems you will ever face / Bernard Heller.— 1st ed.
      p.   cm.
   Includes index.
   ISBN 0-88730-683-7
   1. Commercial correspondence—Handbooks, manuals, etc.   2. Letter writing—Handbooks, manuals, etc.   I. Title.   II. Title: One hundred most difficult business letters you'll ever have to write, fax, or e-mail.
HF5726.H39   1994
651.7'5—dc20   94-5696

94 95 96 97 98   AC/RRD   10 9 8 7 6 5 4 3

DEDICATED TO . . .

The most lovely, lovable, loving ladies of my life:
Pearl . . . Abbe . . . Cynthia . . . Philis

Contents

Acknowledgments

My thanks to the scores of business associates, colleagues, assistants, bosses, and clients—at all levels and in many industries—whom I've closely observed under all conditions of stress and tranquility. They are mentors and models, friends and rivals, shakers and shirkers, dynamic and dinosaurs, and planners and plodders.

Their contours of decision making, their aspirations and drives, their goodness, benevolence, malevolence, egotism, talents, wiles, ways of coping and attainment, and their bright successes and dismal failures have all influenced me. They are, in all, the source material for this book.

My editor, Virginia Smith, is owed my inestimable thanks for her lively understanding, her artful guidance, and quick appreciation of the thrust of this book.

Jane Dystel, my agent, provided consummate judgment and skills that ably piloted this along the right compass heading.

Abbe Heller's insightful views and inspiring judgments were influential in carrying it forward.

Cynthia Flowers contributed savvy comments and perceptions.

Philis Weiss gave me her discerning opinions and erudite grasp of syntax and sense.

Mary Randelman strengthened my resolve to get on with this work, and pointed the way.

Jodi Rivera showed extraordinary skill in deciphering my scribblings, marks, and symbols and putting the material into physical form, page by page. In the same vein, I must credit the expertise of Jacqueline Poli.

Why Did I Decide to Write This Book?

Actually, this book was written dozens of times through the years. I have composed more verbal engagements and discourses than can be counted. I wrote them on demand for clients who needed to persuade, to mollify, to assuage, or to adjure others.

I spent four decades as a hired gun—have pen, will travel—composing presentations, letters, and reports that have made millions for clients. Now, the gleaning, the essence, of all this is between two covers.

What made me decide to write this book? One morning I woke up with the thought that this day I had to write another masterful piece for a client. It was to be a letter. The company was in a spot and the letter had to have the perfect nuance—simple but packed with the right information and the right tone—highly pleasant but showing determination.

Here was another piece that had to make the author look good, win the issue, come out on top. A written communication that could not fail.

How many times does a situation like this arise? More often than not. And when it does the need is critical, and most often eminently stressful.

On that morning the idea was born. . . . Here it is! The first book that understands you are sometimes driven to write an impelling piece. One that has to win the lottery—the first time. You may not get another chance. Yes, writing to win.

Part 1

A CLEAR-CUT STRIDE BEYOND ALL OTHER LETTER-WRITING BOOKS

Section 1 What Is This Book About?

It's about Problem Solving.

About facing up to real-life problems that come up so often. Problems or crises that have to be resolved with a written document.

How many times have you had a pressing need to compose a letter, memo, note, report, or other document about a problem that puts your reputation, your money, or your whole future on the line? One that creates enthusiasm out of lethargy, that nullifies tension or contention—that mitigates an embarrassing circumstance, or that changes people's perceptions. (Keep in mind that perception is reality.)

A business problem in which approval is essential. When "no" could mean a sharp setback, financial hurt, or career-smashing disaster—or when the reader must create actionable interest where none existed before.

And, most often, when there is no second chance. You have to hit a home run the first time at bat. The only time at bat.

When a special kind of written piece is needed, not the same everyday prose.

The letters here are the kinds of communications that can make you come out a winner when it really counts, when there is a stinging penalty for not winning that can range from disquieting to serious to devastating.

How often are business and professional people faced with this kind of need? Consider this question over the course of a year, a month, a week. When this need arises, often without notice, it's besetting and tension-ridden, and it has to be confronted head-on. At times like this you must compose a masterly presentation of your position—with consummate persuasion.

In essence, you have to motivate your reader to respond positively to your agenda. And you have to hit the bull's-eye on the very first shot.

How many smart, capable people get writer's block when they have to sit down to compose a presentation that must energize a favorable response when the chips are down? One that has to communicate clear, concise ideas—softly, simply, without overblown eloquence . . . *and decisively*?

It seems that few people, even those in the highest places, have acquired the technique of composing this special kind of written communication. Unfortunately, a great many don't realize it and continue sending letters—or memos or presentations or reports, or whatever—that are less than effective in giving the extra edge that can mean the difference between success and nonsuccess in winning a crucial point.

Section 2 Why This Is a Different Kind of Business-Writing Book

This is a first-time-ever book, even though there has long been a need for what it teaches. By no means can it be associated with standard letter-writing books, which provide guidance and model letters for prosaic requirements in day-to-day activities. There are many of these, and they serve a useful purpose.

However, these are no help in facing up to invidious, intolerable, and desperate problems that arise, very often when there is no time to deliberate, to ruminate, or to consult. Your nerves are on a hairpin curve, and your written piece must get out in a hurry, frequently the same day.

Up to now there was nothing to turn to that specifically targets workplace vicissitudes, which happen so distressingly often—when a special kind of correspondence is needed; that is, written pieces that require tact, diplomacy, and deft handling, or that capture the attention, the understanding, and the approbation of the reader. The communications to change a state of mind.

Section 3 The Situation—the Strategy—and Then the Written Piece

This book presents over a hundred different problem situations that a reader can relate to—situations that often come up in the course of people's business careers.

Each situation is defined. The definition is followed by a discussion of the strategy to be used in the writing based on an empathetic understanding of the writer's point of view. The discussion then addresses the reasoning, the posture, the tactics, the nuances, and the style that effectively react to the situation.

A prototypical written piece then follows. For the sake of brevity, it is in the form of a letter or memo that suffices to express the words and phrases that convey the strategy and attack the core problem.

A sample report, presentation, or other lengthy discourse would really be an extension of the same strategic solution for the particular problem and would unnecessarily add to the content. The same reasoning and similar phraseology can be lifted for use in lengthier documents.

Prototypical Letters or Memos

The prototype models project varying perspectives and moods of expression corresponding to a strategy or tactic to be used. Each is a riposte to a kind of business problem most people can empathize with. Obviously, this book can't include a written piece to counter every individual situation readers may face. Every need has its individual niceties, its own exquisite distinctions.

A Fertile Source of Ideas and Words

Readers can pick a sample that comes closest to their particular problem. They can glean the ideas, the reasoning, the approach, the meaning, the nuance, and the words and phrases that best suit their intention, that most closely correspond to what they want to say and how they want to say it in their own particular situation.

Fictionalized Depictions of Situations

The models shown here stem from actual circumstances. Names, dates, places, and, in many cases, industries have been changed to conceal identities.

Letters That Count . . . Coming Out Ahead . . . Winning When It's Absolutely, Indubitably Essential

Letters, memos, and so on, in this league must advance the writer's position simply, clearly, and sincerely—without pretension, stuffy rhetoric, or obvious craftiness. The purpose is to make a point, stated in the mood that the writer wants to convey—in the "tone of voice" that elucidates the writer's intent and gets the job done eminently well.

Section
4

What This Book Is Not

This book does not give legal advice or language to stand up in litigation. Legal counsel should be consulted to make certain of airtight protection, if needed, or if adjudication is in the offing. A good lawyer can give the proper sense and key phrases, which if need be can be paraphrased so as to appear casual and friendly—but can carry legal weight if it comes to action that is less cordial.

This book does not countenance fraud, slander, or illegal doings.

It is for pragmatic solutions, not to pursue an evangelical zeal. It is not to hurt people out of glee, to seek pleasure through trickery, or to trip up people as an end in itself. Nor is this a manual on Machiavellian maneuvering as a sport.

This book should not be construed as being of a similar genre as letter books or letter-writing guides published to date. It specifically serves its own unique purpose—to give *career advice* as well as letters.

Nor are these sales letters in the strict sense. This book does not deal with interesting a potential customer in a product or service, nor does it demonstrate how to execute normal customer relations. Plenty of books perform those services.

At Times It's Best Not to Write

Most certainly, there are situations when it's prudent to avoid a written piece. A communication on paper is a documented record, which in some instances should be avoided. There are times when good judgment says, ''Don't put it in writing.'' Common sense will determine whether or not to write as each situation presents itself.

In this, it's good to keep in mind the words of Supreme Court Justice Ruth Bader Ginsburg: ''The written argument endures. The oral argument is fleeting.''

Section
5   # Approaching the Problem

Different Rhymes for Different Times

When it's merely for the record, a humdrum letter or other written piece fills the bill. Why strain for ingenuity when your letter is going to be scanned by a nonentity or the outcome is of little consequence? But, as noted before, presentations to provoke an action or change an attitude require an extra dynamism.

Play Hardball . . . Play Softball . . . Choose What the Game Calls For.

Start with Strategy

Think of your communication piece as a strategic plan of action—a battle plan to accomplish your goal. Next, pick the weapon you must use—that is, the message you compose.

First, decide what you want the end result to be and zero in on the central idea you want to implant in the mind of the reader. Other points may serve a good purpose, but in general view them as embellishing or supportive. (There are, of course, exceptions to this rule.)

It's difficult enough to sell one idea in a single document, let alone several. Besides, approval of the key proposition is the ace that will win the game.

Be pragmatic about determining the ultimate result you set in your sights. It's best not to reach ridiculously high, grasping for what is realistically unattainable. It could make your whole premise seem ludicrous.

Nor do you want your sincerity impeached by appearing disingenuous or with any hint of being duplicitous or Machiavellian. True-blue earnestness must be projected. Common sense is your guide.

Set the Pace to Make the Case

Now you have to decide on the battle tactics and the weaponry for carrying out your strategic plan. Your written piece is a weapon.

Determine the Mood . . . Are you in a position to assume a confident, assertive stance, or must you adjure the goodwill of the recipient—or perhaps adopt a middle ground?

For example, should you be threatening or defensive, friendly or formal, negotiable or resolute, sedate or whimsical?

Use the Right Tone of Voice . . . Examples: angry but composed, appealing without begging, happy without gushing, complying without surrendering, forceful without stridency, joy without treacle, correcting without disparaging, or certainty without dogmatism.

In short, pick the strategy, then design the thrust to make it happen.

A Crucial Determinant Is the Key Factor—LEVERAGE

What do you have working for you or against you? What's the atmosphere that overhangs the issue?

The ultimate leverage is having logic, law, good sense, and clout on your side. How close are you to this ideal? Which of these advantages can you muster? How much muscle can you flex?

Keep It Simple, Straightforward

It should be in plain English, no-nonsense straight talk, but polished and correct, in an easy-to-grasp style. Above all, be sincere. You have to believe in your proposition. Keep in mind that you are asking for the reader's trust.

Avoid at all costs the stiff bureaucratese that's so prevalent today. You can get away with it in international diplomatic circles or within legislative councils, but it will get you a loud ho-hum in this league.

There should be no sense of seeking plaudits for erudition or bombastic eloquence, nor for vanity or intellectual games. Above all, include no gratuitous cynicism. Remember, your express intention is to build consensus and harmony around your position.

Be as certain as possible that your facts and numbers are justifiable. Very little can do more harm to a document than getting caught with a factual error or fallacious reasoning. You can be sure that some will love to seize on it.

Timing—Essential to Raise Your Potential

Speed increases the impact of your message. Get it out while the event is fresh in everyone's mind. Otherwise, it can be a thing of the past, overtaken by more immediate interests.

Very often, there is little time to ponder over the right approach, the right words. It's at such times that a reference guide such as this is so essential. To get started right, compose a winning document, score a hit.

Do It—Do It Again and Again Until You're Confident It's Right—but Don't Be Bogged Down by Indecisiveness

You might want to write an outline of the strategy as a guide, especially in a complex situation. This step also assigns a continuity to the various points you are making.

Now for your first draft. Write it the way you want to say it. It may come out fairly close to perfect on the first try, but don't count on it. It hardly ever happens.

Next comes the fine-tuning. Sharpen it, correct the syntax and grammar. Defog, simplify, and eliminate needless or ineffective words. Many people go through this process four or five times or more. You'll instinctively know when your document will fly.

Good grammar is obviously important—but keep in mind that English is a living, growing language. Your basic purpose is to communicate in an interesting way so that people will want to read what you have to say, so that your thesis is crystal clear, and so that it makes you look good, bright, and right.

Bland is a block. Intricate is an enemy. Petulance signals retreat. Inexplicitness will lay you low. Dull will kill.

This Is Your Opportunity. Don't Blow It. History Rarely Grants a Second Chance.

Enjoy and Revel. Be a Black Belt Contestant in High-Stakes Business Writing.

Now—here's a weapon to help you create letters, memos, and presentations to sell a premise or make a case—to activate, simplify, reinforce, redress, or optimize.

The skills this book teaches will show you how to write a written piece that communicates in a way that is right for the problem at hand. Your letters will crackle, sting, jab, smile, or purr, as the case may be. This is writing to impel, to gain approval—to win for the pleasure of winning, the reward of winning, the necessity to win, and to win when not winning is unthinkable.

This is the subtle, facile power this book brings to your playing field of human relations.

Part 2

PROTOTYPE LETTERS AND MEMOS

Understandably, the letters and memos here cannot explicitly apply to every single situation or problem that all readers encounter. It goes without saying that every need has its individual niceties, its unique shadings. Thus, these prototypes relate to typical situations.

Look at them as case studies.

Pick out the letters that come closest to your purpose. Select from these the approach, the nuance, the meaning that fits your strategy. Cull phrases or paragraphs that suit your intention. Glean the words you find appropriate. There may be times when you can lift a letter in its entirety.

Clearly, here's a source of ideas to give you a decided edge in persuading, in creating empathy, in bringing the thoughts and intent that are in your mind into the mind of the person you are addressing . . . to cope, to overcome, to obtain support, to achieve your objective . . . to be effective.

**Select, enjoy, and thrive from
this bountiful cornucopia of ideas.**

Your Ideas . . . Protect Them from Being Usurped. Advance, Support, Promote Them.

Make Sure You Get Full Credit for Your Ideas.

Situation: You are a marketing executive in a surgical supply company. The sales climate is changing rapidly. Your company is struggling to maintain its market share as new, agile competitors shoulder their way into the marketplace.

In addition, you are trying to adjust to recent structural changes in hospital and HMO purchasing procedures. It means you have to modify your data-processing and billing framework, a daunting job. In addition, you have to realign your sales strategy to adequately service these important classes of trade.

How to cope and move ahead was the subject of a brainstorming meeting, moderated by the chief executive officer. Ideas were bandied about, hashed, rehashed, and dashed. You had a few stunning ideas that you took the time to think through before the meeting.

Considering the tumultuous session that took place, your ideas stand a good chance of emerging much altered, if they survive at all. At the least, they will lose your stamp and be credited to the group, not to you personally.

You came up with some of the best solutions, but there will be no glory for your brilliance and toil.

Strategy: Send a memo to the moderator, copies to the rest of the group. And a copy to the chairman, who was not at the meeting.

Explain your ideas thoroughly and in detail. It is to be your explanation of these ideas as you voiced them originally, not what came out of the communal group. Now it will be on the record as coming from you. You rightfully give your assistant credit for the idea he had suggested.

This is a forthright showing of integrity, and it stamps your name even deeper on the other gems you are listing.

The format is a covering letter outlining each of these ideas in brief, which will serve to claim credit for each of them. Attached to this are detailed descriptions of each one.

**IN-HOUSE MEMO TO YOUR COLLEAGUES,
COPY TO THE CHAIRMAN**

February 13, 1994

To: Diana Horsman St. Lucia
      Karl DeEhmer
      Jeanie Felton
      Harold Scott
      Catherine Victor
      Mr. C. Everett Fifer, Chairman

From: Sie Chin

Re: 1/25/94 Brainstorming Meeting—Tackling the New Competition for Hospital and HMO Business.

Many things were bandied about at our meeting, and everyone, it seems, came up with really good suggestions, including some ingenious ideas that I believe should be taken off our notepads and put to practical use. They are too good to be left dangling. Wasn't this the purpose of the meeting?

I've gotten some further insights on the ideas I had submitted, and I think it's best to put this on paper, since we may not meet in another such session for some time.

This is the gist of the ideas I offered. A detailed explanation of each one is on the pages that follow.

1. An association with a major pharmaceutical manufacturer to jointly open up and service new hospital and HMO accounts in major markets.

2. Self-study courses for doctors that will grant them continuing education credits. They are to deal, of course, with the diseases in which we are involved.

3. Working hand in hand with inner-city groups and local governments on health and nutrition problems. This will give us a favored entree to public hospitals and medicaid plans. We will be in a preferred position for huge volume potential.

4. Product education seminars for personnel at major medical centers, HMOs, and VA hospitals.

Number 4 is the idea of my assistant, Bob McDonald, and I want to give him full credit.

                                        Regards,

                                        Sie Chin

Get Your Brilliant Idea Past the Hierarchical Minefields for a Fair Hearing at the Top. Overcome the "Not Invented Here" Syndrome.

Situation: You were a sales representative for a data communications company, recently laid off because of a severe retrenchment. Now you are on your own as an independent sales promotion consultant.

You have a blockbuster idea for a long-distance phone company. It will substantially increase their business. It's an entirely new concept that entails joint ventures with major travel companies and other entities to tap into their customers when they take a pleasure tour or a business trip. It will benefit both the phone company and its joint-venture partners.

You had previously done promotional work for a long-distance provider, which gave you valuable insight into this business. You know their needs, and you know the competitive strengths and weaknesses of the leading players in this combative industry.

You have spoken to the marketing people at three potential partner prospects. You didn't reveal the full concept, but you gave sufficient information so as to be able to gauge their attitude. They were all extremely positive. In fact, enthusiastic.

From all this background, your idea materialized into a tangible, practical design for greatly expanding a phone company's customer base of frequent long-distance users.

You now have a wonderful idea that can make money for you by means of setting up the procedure and helping to run it as a consultant. That is, if the company will go along.

Strategy: Now, how to get a good hearing at a phone company that has the facilities, the resources, and the bankroll to make your idea blossom into a sustained, full-scale campaign? And where you will be handsomely rewarded for your ingenuity and your ability to get this done.

How do you make the approach?

Select your primary target—and targets two, three, and four.

Where do you have a friend, or a friend of a friend, who can give you the corporate intelligence you need—the personalities, the decision makers, the doers, the formal and informal hierarchy, the sensors on what and who to avoid? This person should be a good starting point, someone who can ease you in, whether it be company one, two, or three—or perhaps number four as you go down the line.

If you have no such champion, you'll have to devise your own approach. Why not start with the company that can make the loudest noise, the one with the deep pockets? Are they likely to take a chance on something new? Likely to test-market the concept?

You have to come in from the cold and penetrate the glass wall of obstructionism, even enmity, against alien ideas that shoulder in from beyond the company's sheltered confines. You will be regarded as a threat to the establishment, to be sniped at, not embraced.

After all, sales ideas are what they, or their various ad and sales promotion agencies, are paid to think up. A foreign idea, especially if it is good, becomes a personal threat. Very few feel secure enough to brook such intrusions from an out-of-the-way source.

A subtle way of fending off interlopers such as you is to declare the idea, or an offshoot of it, as having already been considered at some time in the past. In other words, it is not new to them, and it can't work for some reason.

Then again, one idea breeds another, and you may see the intrinsic germ of your creation introduced at some later time, altered or fabricated so that the company is able to disclaim any outside authorship.

How do you push the hot button to get in from the cold?

Several approaches can be considered.

1. Call and send a letter to the CEO or the senior marketing executive.

   You may well be ignored completely. Then again, you may receive a short, respectful response from an underling, noting that .the company doesn't consider ideas from outside sources. Or they may ask you to get in touch with another (lower-level) executive who is concerned with such things. Or maybe your letter is being directed to a junior executive, who will get in touch with you.

   All of the above is the kiss of death.

   The executive who has been "annoyed" with your request for a hearing may call and have you explain your idea on the phone or ask that you come in for a meeting.

   The meeting more than likely will be with the marketing staff who will, with due respect, carefully lower your idea to the grave for the aforementioned "not invented here" reason.

2. Another entry avenue is through their advertising, sales-promotion, or direct-marketing supplier—the people who are hired to come up with selling ideas.

   You'll have to share the glory, but half is better than none. And in this way, you will have a cheerleader fronting for you. Needless to say, their motive is to get the credit for discerning a good idea and bringing it to their client. Nevertheless, you are still known as the author and will profit from your input and implementation.

3. Another way is to contact an outside member of the board of directors. Send a letter stating you have a well-conceived concept for increasing the company's business. Request that it be directed to the proper person at the company.

   The board member likely has no ax to grind and feels duty bound to see that anything that can help the company gets exposed to the people who are supposed to act on it.

The board member may send your letter along to the CEO or a high executive and suggest they contact you. He/she may also send you the name of the person to see. You then send a letter to this person or persons saying that you were asked by Ms. Theresa Madalone, a member of the board of directors, to get in touch with them because you have a concept that Ms. Madalone thinks warrants serious consideration.

If you don't get a decent review by the company's people, write the board member again, saying that the company doesn't appear to be interested in good ideas that can help raise their profits. At the least, they should give you a serious hearing. Isn't this their job?

If you want to get more extreme, buy a few shares of the company's stock and pose as an irate shareholder.

The board member may want to dispose of this matter, get it off his or her back, and present your case to the CEO or chairman. "Aren't you guys interested in seeing something that may be good for the company? It shouldn't be dismissed just because it's from someone on the outside."

You may have to sign a waiver prior to a meeting at the company. It will protect the company from any claims you may make of usurping your idea if the company had thought of something like it before you presented it. Effectively, you will have a hard time claiming authorship if the company appropriates the essence of your concept or alters it while retaining the core benefit.

If they make the waiver a condition to seeing what you have, you will have to sign it—but add a clause giving you some protection.

The aforementioned are some suggested methods of entry. You may bump into others as you pursue your campaign. The situation is fluid. Things may come up that give you a lead to follow.

You must be persistent—and patience is essential regardless of your frustration. Above all, make sure your presentation is superlative. Preparation, preparation. Be always mindful to be respectful of everyone you see or hear. Everyone, from the top down. And you must command respect from everyone. Good luck!

LETTER TO A SENIOR MARKETING EXECUTIVE AT THE COMPANY YOU ARE APPROACHING

February 18, 1994

Mr. Wendell Josephs
Vice President, Marketing
Northern Telephone, Inc.

_____

_____

Dear Mr. Josephs:

> "Four things come not back—the spoken word, the sped arrow,
> the past life, and the neglected opportunity." (Arabian proverb)

I have formulated and researched a marketing idea that will significantly benefit Northern Telephone, which I would be most happy to present to you.

No long-distance company, including Northern, has ever executed this kind of promotion. It is unique. And it has great promise of significantly increasing your long-distance sales and market share.

Briefly, it is designed to enlarge Northern's credit card base among the most frequent long-distance users, with special emphasis on switching competitive phone customers. In fact, it will strengthen the competitive standing of any large long-distance provider.

I have been a marketing consultant for the past 10 years and have originated a number of successful marketing programs for several giant companies. And I am experienced in long-distance marketing, so I know your industry quite well.

Northern Telephone is my first choice in making this presentation, primarily because of your creativity and keen marketing sense in recognizing an original idea of exceptional merit and giving it the proper thrust to assure success. I'm aware of your reputation on this score, which is why I'm writing to you.

I suggest that we meet to go over this. If you wish, however, I will send you a written description prior to our meeting, with the understanding, of course, that the information is privileged.

Very truly yours,

LETTER TO THE ACCOUNT SUPERVISOR AT THE COMPANY'S AD AGENCY

February 18, 1994

Ms. Elizabeth Bard Buckley
Vice President, Account Supervisor
Abbot, Hellman, O'Neill Advertising Co.

_____

_____

Dear Ms. Buckley:

> "Each thought that is welcomed and recorded is a nest egg,
>   by the side of which more will be laid." (Thoreau)

I would like to share an idea with you that's in the interest of your client, Northern Telephone. It's a promotional system to increase Northern's credit card customer base and encourage their use of the credit card for long-distance calls. It is specially designed to switch competitive long-distance customers. The idea can benefit any long-distance company, including Northern's closest competitors. But I prefer to bring it to you first.

In short, this concept is not merely a sudden flash of inspiration. Nor is it a simple germ of an idea. It's a carefully thought out and well-researched promotional plan, a stunning new concept for increasing Northern's share of the long-distance market. It can lead to a whole new advertising and promotional campaign. And it can be easily tested.

The concept involves partner relationships with certain major companies who have indicated a desire to seriously explore this kind of arrangement.

I have been a sales communications consultant for ten years and have originated a number of money-making concepts for several giant corporations.

There is, of course, the alternative of going directly to your client. But I prefer to present it to you first, since I'm aware of your reputation as having a very talented eye for exceptional selling ideas—and knowing how to make them work. And, in fact, you personally are quite famous for originating such sales concepts for Northern.

Let's get together and talk about it. I'm confident that you'll find it to be a great service to Northern and will want to get behind it. If you wish, I can describe it in writing prior to our meeting.

                                        Regards,

LETTER TO AN OUTSIDE MEMBER OF THE
BOARD OF DIRECTORS

February 18, 1994

Ms. G. Theresa Madalone
Member of the Board of Directors
Northern Telephone Co.
c/o Furlong Industries, Inc.

_____

_____

Dear Ms. Madalone:

> "So long as new ideas are created, sales will
> continue to reach new highs." (Charles F. Kettering)

May I ask your assistance in presenting a remarkable sales development concept—an eye-opening new opportunity for Northern Telephone.

I say this as an individual who has been in the marketing business for a long time, with a strong knowledge of long-distance marketing. I am willing to turn this over to Northern for their serious assessment. I am not representing a company or group.

The idea I am able to present has been carefully structured and researched, including a thorough examination of Northern's previous promotional campaigns. Northern has never done anything like this, nor has any other phone company.

In a nutshell, it is designed to significantly increase Northern's credit card base among frequent long-distance users, with special emphasis on switching competitive phone customers. In fact, it could elevate the market share of any of the major long-distance companies.

I'm asking if you would be good enough to steer me to the proper person at Northern who is responsible for their marketing plans and is in a position to introduce this concept if he or she finds it fitting.

If you wish, in advance of a meeting at Northern, I'll be pleased to describe the thrust of this idea to you in a written document or meet with you to discuss it.

Very truly yours,

FOLLOW-UP TO THE BOARD MEMBER IF THE COMPANY REFUSES TO REVIEW YOUR IDEA

March 3, 1994

Ms. G. Theresa Madalone
Member of the Board of Directors
Northern Telephone Co.
c/o Furlong Industries, Inc.

_____

_____

Dear Ms. Madalone:

You will recall that I requested the name of the right person at Northern Telephone who can evaluate and act on the sales enhancement concept that I developed.

It was good of you to give me the name of Mr. Wendell Josephs, vice president of marketing, to whom I've written. I sent a copy of the letter to Mr. Theodore McGracken, CEO.

However, regretfully—for me, and I should add for Northern as well—I received a rather curt negative response. Speaking as a stockholder, I'm sure you share my concern that the people at Northern feel so complacent about their business that they don't care to even look at a marketing concept that may be of inestimable value. I say this as a professional marketing consultant with a background in the long-distance industry.

Northern, as everyone knows, is in a highly volatile and very competitive market. I don't believe their people are in a position to ignore what could be a powerful sales strategy that can strengthen their competitive position.

Thank you so much, Ms. Madalone, for the help you've given me to date. Perhaps you can guide me on pursuing this further with Northern. It seems that Northern should thank you as well.

Truly yours,

Prior to presenting your idea to the company, they may ask you to sign a waiver disclaiming original authorship if the company previously knew of the concept from another source.

In this case, a statement such as this should be appended.

I am signing this waiver with the understanding that other sales-building ideas that Northern Telephone may have conceived, and which are in their files, may possibly have certain similarities to the one I'm presenting. However, this is not a valid claim of proprietorship if such ideas do not have the same unique and original features.

Your Seminal Idea Was Approved by a Client. But Nothing Was Done About It. Get It Going.

Two situations:

I. The ideas are presented to a company on a free-lance basis. There is no formal client relationship.

II. The ideas are presented to a valuable client under a client–agency contract.

Situation I: Your company, a marketing communications enterprise, came up with a powerful idea to substantially increase subscriptions to a magazine that's been around for a long time and is still popular, but inching downward. You developed a unique concept to reverse this baleful trend and breathe new life into the publication. Acting as a free-lance consultant, you presented it to the publishing and editorial staffs. It was unanimously acknowledged as a bright new concept that is just the ticket for reviving the publication. The palpable message was *go,* and the staff personnel were to meet among themselves on timing and details.

Six weeks have passed and you haven't heard anything of substance. Where is the former enthusiasm? A great deal of time and money was spent on this proposal. You must know if it will fly.

Strategy I: You urge them to formally tell you whether they will make your concept operational, and if so, when. You advise them of your option to take it elsewhere if it is turned down or remains in a nether world much longer.

YOUR IDEA WAS PRESENTED FREE-LANCE

September 27, 1994

Mr. Henry Wisniak
President and Publisher
Merriwether Publications

Re: Follow-up to meeting of 8/9—Ideas for X12 Project

Dear Hank:

The meeting was a great success. Everyone thought our idea for renewals and new subscriptions was marvelous. Jerry Tramiel used the word "incredible." It wasn't my word, but I happen to agree with Jerry.

You were also very gung ho, noting it as an innovative coordination of telemarketing, direct mail and integrative TV, with a creative copy concept—all designed to give birth to a superpowerful campaign.

That was six weeks ago, and we haven't heard anything from you or your people. Our phone calls didn't get any substantive response. You know as well as anyone, Hank, that ideas don't come easily. Good ideas are valuable. Great money-making ideas are precious.

We really have to know how it stands. If you still want to make your target launch date, we have to clear our decks now because there's a tremendous amount of up-front work to be done.

If you are still serious about the program but are holding it up for a later date, let us know so we can rearrange our in-house work schedules. Or, perhaps if it is far down the line, we may consider taking this idea elsewhere, after discussing this option with you.

On the other hand, we need to know if you have abandoned the program or it is in an indefinite hiatus. In this event, we will be free to present it to another publisher as soon as feasible. It goes without saying that we will not divulge any confidential information you gave us.

I realize you and your staff are swamped right now. But can you please give us an answer soon, say by October 15?

Thanks, Hank, I'm looking forward to hearing from you, and most of all, working with you on this stunning breakthrough project.

Regards,

Situation II: Your direct-marketing agency is under contract to a leading magazine publisher to create and implement circulation enhancement programs. The title you service has a circulation of over a million, which has been slowly eroding for years.

Your company was given the assignment of turning it around and came up with an ingenious method of stopping the skid and moving circulation in the right direction. It was presented to the publishing and editorial staffs and was given its rightful accolades. There was every indication of getting this project into high gear promptly. "This is what we're looking for" was the clear message—or so you thought.

It's now six weeks later, and the idea has been lingering in your client's confines. There has been no definite word despite your specific, yet deferential, prodding. This is a valuable client, and they must not be irked. There must be no risk of alienation.

Strategy II: Write a normal company–client letter, respectful but to the point. Ask about the status of your recommendation, noting that it got an exuberant go-ahead reception.

You need to know because you require about a month's notice to tool up, and it is getting close to the most opportune launch date.

YOUR IDEA WAS PRESENTED TO A VALUABLE CLIENT

September 27, 1994

Mr. Henry Wisniak
President and Publisher
Merriwether Publications

_____

_____

Re: Follow-up to 8/9 Meeting—Recommended Plan for X12 Project

Dear Hank:

I am bringing this up because there has been no decision as yet about this project, and we may miss out on the most advantageous launching date. We had agreed, I believe, that it should be in the early fall. We need at least four weeks to tool up.

It's hard to keep an innovative idea like this under wraps for long, especially with the possibility of leaks. So the sooner we go to work, the better off we'll all be.

Imagine how we'd feel if we saw another publisher start a campaign like this, or even one that's pretty close. We would be chastising ourselves for not moving ahead when we had the chance. Let's make sure we keep this jewel for ourselves and get a good step ahead of the competition.

I recently came across this quote from Thomas Kennedy, the author: "Ideas lose themselves as quickly as quail, and one must wing them the minute they rise out of the grass—or they are gone."

I'll call you to find out the status. With the hope, please, that we will decide on a starting date.

Best regards,

Actuate Your Marvelous Proposal. It Never Reached Top Management, Because a Company Committee Nitpicked It to Death.

Two strategies:

I. Come out swinging.

II. Walk softly, diplomatically.

Situation: A power utility has been getting a lot of flak from the community it serves because of service problems and certain overcharges. The local politicos have taken it up as a cause.

You gathered the forces in your department, with the help of other specialists in the company. You worked on it for weeks with little sleep. Here was a high-profile chance to show what you can do. You could be a hero. When all your ducks were in a row, you made an all-out presentation to the committee.

The chairman of the utility set up an ad hoc coordinating committee of four top-level executives to solve the problem and get a 180-degree turnaround of the public's hostility, which is driven by the media. As director of corporate communications, the committee assigned you to come up with an effective plan of action—what to do, how to do it, and how to make sure it works. This is a tough mandate. The plan *has* to work; there is no second chance.

Your plan was creative, stunning, and forceful. Some operational factors didn't hang together neatly, but these were minuscule details that could be straightened out before the plan goes into play.

The committee seized on the small operational trivialities that needed fixing. They nitpicked it without mercy to an agonizing annihilation. They didn't make the BIG IDEA the center of discussion and focus on how it can help the company. Instead, they ridiculed the minutiae, even though they didn't mar the strength and beauty of the overall plan. It was like demolishing an exquisite building because the elevators were too slow.

You suspect that there was some underlying jealousy in all this. This innovative, daring stroke would be a publicist's dream. There would be good press, which would undoubtedly single you out as the originator. You would be the fair-haired boy, upstaging the executives on the committee.

You can't let this die. The plan is too good, and the issue you are solving is vitally important to the utility and to the community—not to mention your career.

Strategy I: You are sure you can safely go over the heads of the committee members and right to the chairman. The very top. Your plan is your best ally.

Write him a letter or memo. You have to be forceful to make your point and get a good second chance to score. You also have to be unqualifiedly sure of yourself, which you are.

Go to it. Don't worry about ruffling egos. You are convinced your position is too good for you to lose. And there is so much to gain.

COME OUT SWINGING IN A COMPLAINT TO
THE CHAIRMAN

August 9, 1994

To: Mr. H. Peter Kennedy, Chairman
        Hampton Power & Light

From: Clarisa Gardineaux

"There has never been a statue set up in honor of a critic." So said Jean Sibelius, the Finnish composer.

The reason is that critics have a significant place, but they are not doers. Doers make the wheels spin. They innovate successful programs. They cause growth and profits, year after year.

My department managers and I worked day and night for a total of about a hundred hours each on the community service plan I presented to the Can-Do Committee on Friday.

Hours spent are not a criteria of how good a piece of work is, of course. But this plan has tremendous merit. It will speed up our service to our consumers, greatly improve relations with our big customers, and be a focus for wonderful public relations coverage.

The committee asked us for a concrete plan. We gave it to them. Certainly, there are details that have to be worked out, little knots that have to be untangled. This can be done with the help of the rest of the company staff. That is, if there is a willingness to put it on the company do-now schedule.

This plan is good. It will work. I exposed it to some of the people in other departments. They raved about its spunk and potential. We all agreed it needed some smoothing out here and there, but these are trivial details, which don't lessen the worth of the plan itself. The ingenuity of the idea as a means of solving our problem is valid. This is what counts.

It was not an open-minded committee that I made my presentation to. It was an adversarial session. They condemned it for these little, insignificant things rather than seeing what the big picture looks like.

We are asking that this be reviewed again. Give us a chance. Give this company a chance to fix a vexing problem and at the same time show its ingenuity and demonstrate how well it carries out its civic responsibility.

Respectfully,

Clarisa Gardineaux
Clarisa Gardineaux

Strategy II: You follow the old adage: "You can sell anything if you don't mind sharing the credit." You know that the four committee members, all major executives, will get the glory, or most of it.

Write them a memo with copy to the chairman saying that their help is necessary to get the plan operational. Only they can get it on track by smoothing out the rough spots. They can then turn the ignition on the public relations steamroller. The committee members will share the acclaim with the chairman.

You know the esteem will come to you eventually. You are recognized as the one who devised the idea and brought it full bloom to the committee. The chairman knows it, and your coworkers know it. It will surely be leaked to the press.

WALK SOFTLY AND DIPLOMATICALLY IN A MEMO TO THE COMMITTEE

August 9, 1994

To: The Operation Can-Do Committee
        Lawrence Burnham
        Josephine Engelhart
        Harold Goodman
        Anita Rosenzweig

From: Clarisa Gardineaux

c.c.   Mr. H. Peter Kennedy, Chairman

I'm grateful to the ad hoc committee and to each of you individually for pointing out certain operational problems with the plan I presented. I think we all agree that these are details—important ones to be sure—that can be easily fixed. When this is done the plan will be a roaring success.

The creative way you quickly realized what needs to be done points us in a clear direction for successfully solving the company's problem. No other utility company in the country has done anything like this, which makes a fertile field for some really great publicity.

You indicated what the bugs are. Now we need your ingenuity in getting them out and getting the program onto the drawing board. This will be great for the company as well as the community we serve.

It would also be good if you set the pace in getting media coverage. The company can get a lot of glory out of this. But I think it's appropriate that you, collectively and as individuals, be the spokespersons. Along with Mr. Kennedy, of course.

Thanks so much, and it's a remarkable experience working for you.

                Regards,

                Clarisa Gardineaux
                Clarisa Gardineaux

Your Work Gets "Corrected" and Censored, Changing It from Great to Mediocre.

Situation: You are a network TV producer working on a hot new program concept. The person responsible for standards and clearance is far more careful and conscientious than necessary. He cuts and slashes the script to the point where the audience interest will be stunted. You are convinced this timidity will make the program a bomb instead of a smash hit.

Strategy: Send him a strong but chummy memo with copies to the production chief and head of marketing saying that he's going too far. You note that the network can have ample protection without tearing the guts out of the script.

IN-HOUSE MEMO TO THE "CENSOR"

August 14, 1993

To: Jerry Turno
        Vice President, Internal Affairs and Program Clearance

From: Maggie Blackstone

Re: The "What Went Wrong?" Show . . . Slated for fall lineup.

c.c.   Abbe Hill Curtin
        George Mopilos

Jerry, I well understand you have to be sure that we don't get pilloried by the people who are mentioned in the program, are not subject to any libel suits, avoid gratuitous sexual overtones, etc. As the guardian of this company's welfare and wealth, you have an acute responsibility, which I well understand.

However, it goes without saying that the company has to get out shows that attract audiences. As such, they must be timely, of blockbuster interest, and often provocative.

I understand your caution, but all I ask is that you reconsider some of the changes you called for in the scripts. Your omissions and disclaimers emasculate its interest, its excitement, the kind of talk-about we want, the publicity, and the reviews we hope for. In short, the ratings and the advertising sales.

Jerry, can't you pull in most of your changes and still have ample protection? You are excising the muscle and guts from the scripts.

It's like extracting all the teeth to prevent cavities.

                                        Cordially,

                                        Maggie Blackstone

Your Client Gives Your Ideas to Their Other Agent. Stop It.

Situation: You are a partner at a financial services company. Your function is to develop ideas for financial swaps and new equity placements. You have done this for one of your highly rated clients. However, you discovered that they are now implementing an especially praiseworthy financial plan you had presented six months ago—but not with you. A rival financial house is making money and getting good publicity from your idea.

Strategy: Write a letter to your client pointing out your displeasure, but not so harshly as to cause ill feeling. You don't want to jeopardize the relationship, yet the letter has to impart a clear-cut notification that this must not go on.

LETTER TO YOUR CLIENT

December 3, 1993

James T. Reilly
Senior Vice President
Boomer Products, Inc.

_____

_____

Dear Jim:

This deals generally with the producing of IDEAS, one of the most important functions that we are privileged to provide for you. As such, it specifically discusses something that came up recently that is somewhat disturbing.

We value your account to a great extent, and we get great satisfaction out of the harmonious way we work together. One of the reasons is the way you encourage us to give vent to our ideas—ideas that help your business. And ours too, indirectly, of course.

You appreciate a good idea when you see one. You know how to adapt an idea to your needs better than anyone I've ever known. That's why you inspire us. In short, you provide a lush environment for creativity.

Jim, you know more than anyone that good ideas are hard to come by. We strain. We research. We review. We argue, often into the night. We hope that when an idea is accepted, we'll implement it for you and make a valuable property out of it so that you will make a lot of money on it. . . . And we'll make some, too.

So it was disturbing—and I must say, frustrating—when we saw one of the ideas we presented to you six months ago now being carried out by Boomer. Not with us, but with another shop.

Even though what we saw was practically what we presented, they might have thought of it independently. It happens sometimes. If that's so in this case, I apologize for mentioning it.

This is nothing very serious. I just wanted to let you know how we feel around here. We love handling your issues, and we're proud to have you as a client. You know we'll give you the best service and the best ideas in the business.

Cordially,

Your Highly Acclaimed Marketing Project Is Floundering on Your Client's Back Burner. Move It Up Front and Put a Fire Under It.

Situation: You are a principal at an ad agency supervising a world-class health-care account. You have presented an innovative sales-building plan that was applauded by all as a startling concept. All signals called for moving ahead with gusto. That was six months ago, but nothing has happened.

   All the people involved have been busy with ongoing projects while this marketing gem is relegated to the back burner. For the good of the company, the starting switch has to be turned on.

Strategy: Send a letter to the company's marketing chief, who has this project in his bailiwick. It must prod him to start the action without seeming too critical of his past stalling.

LETTER TO YOUR CLIENT

October 13, 1993

Conrad D. Van Devander
Executive Vice President, Marketing
Denoyer Health Care, Ltd.

_____

_____

cc: Roger Baldwin
     Dorothy Su
     Lindsey Schreiber

Dear Conrad:

What a great idea! Just what we need! It will demolish our competition!

This is what was said six months ago, when the agency presented our business-building plan for Nemenosa 3. You'll recall we had it all buttoned up, ready to go. We said it would take three months to get this operational, and we were virtually told to get ready for a test in four states. But the go button wasn't pressed.

Since then, we did as much as we could to keep it moving: letters, meetings, reminders. But everyone—and it goes for your people and ours—has been so bogged down on immediate projects that they couldn't spend time on this, as important as it is.

As you often said, Conrad, the business depends on forward thinking. We presented an exciting, forward-thinking plan that was accepted without question. Six months have passed, and there is still no forward involvement. We can't afford to allow this to languish.

Imagine how we would all feel if a competitor came out with a similar marketing program. Think of how foolish we'd all look. It would be tragic. We must be absolutely sure this doesn't happen.

Conrad, your people do a wonderful job, and ours do, too. We work well together. Let's get the Nemenosa 3 business builder off the back burner now. Now's the time to put your finger on the go button.

Best wishes to Clara and the kids,

Phil Cleary

Phil Cleary

Prevent a Prospective Client from Stealing an Idea You Are Presenting.

Situation: Your company, Sales Promotion, Inc., is going to present an innovative sales-boosting idea to Ideal Vacations, Inc. It will be a good piece of business for you if they buy it. The relationship is such that it would not be judicious to put a legalistic protection agreement in front of them to sign. They probably would call off the meeting. At best, they would consult their lawyer, which would hold up the presentation. It will then become a legal-maneuvering game.

You are anxious to get going with them, but you want to claim that you own the idea and tactfully state that they would have a problem if it's used without your involvement.

Strategy: Have a letter to show preceding your presentation. It should be the front page of the bound write-up you leave with them. It must say that the idea is your property and that you are the one to implement it, which, incidentally, is to their benefit as well as yours.

The letter should point up the business-building value of your idea. It was done in the presentation, but reiterate this point anyway. You must give it the hype it deserves.

Indicate that you are exposing this idea to them as your first choice. But, understandably, it will be presented to a competitor if they turn it down.

You must keep in mind that this may not necessarily give you ironclad legal protection. It establishes you as the innovator and could strengthen your case if they steal the idea from you and you choose to take legal action.

LETTER ACCOMPANYING YOUR PRESENTATION

September 15, 1993

Ideal Vacations, Inc.

————————————————————

————————————————————

Attn: Gordon Sessions, Senior Vice President
        Tomaso Estrada, Vice President
        Virginia Hooper, Vice President

Here's our presentation of the business-building plan we discussed with you. It is being made to Ideal exclusively at this time.

Based on our projections, which are backed up by our research data, we're confident you will add 10 to 15 percent in sales above your normal volume in the first year following the introduction of this promotion.

In effect, you will build a bigger sales base and increase your market share.

The basic marketing idea and operational procedures in the presentation are confidential and proprietary to Sales Promotion, Inc. If you elect to implement this program, the promotional campaign and data processing are to be supervised by our company under Ideal's direction.

As you can imagine, we put months of time and a great deal of out-of-pocket expense plus a good amount of creative thinking into the task of developing this marketing idea and its implementation. Sales Promotion, Inc., is undoubtedly in the best position to launch the program and keep it running successfully.

Now to an important point, which I'm sure you agree with. This startling new vacation concept will create tremendous noise in the travel market and give you a big leg up on your competition. There will likely be copycats, but you'll have the clear benefit that goes with being first. You'll be out front with the strongest promotion concept in many years.

Very truly,

Stephen Mandel

Stephen Mandel
President

Fight Back at an Idea Thief. Your Brilliant Concept Was Appropriated by the Company You Presented It to.

Situation: You are the owner of a direct-marketing company. You devised a new concept for switching customers from one brand of a packaged-goods product to another. Better yet, the acquired customers are encouraged to stay with the product they switched to and not go back to their former brand. In other words, it is a long-range business-building campaign for a packaged-goods company. It's done by means of a multimedia program using telemarketing, direct mail, and advertising.

You whetted the interest of marketing executives at a big liquor company. You knew this approach would be a superb marketing tool for a whiskey brand. That's why you contacted them. They agreed to see what you had, and you made a formal presentation.

They went for it, or so it seemed to you. It was right, they said, for their vodka product, which needed a shot in the arm, so to speak. Still a big seller, this brand was gradually losing market share. You left two bound presentations behind. They said they'd get back.

There was no signed confidentiality agreement. You trusted them. Frankly, if you had insisted on such an agreement, you likely would not have had the meeting.

During the next four months or so, some of the liquor people called with questions but no commitments. Eight months after your presentation, you saw something that gave you a fifty-point blood pressure surge. The company has put your concept—or its clone—out in the marketplace, supported by a big ad campaign. It's being done through their regular ad agency. Everything you see tells you it's an out-and-out theft of your idea.

Strategy: You don't want to run to high-priced legal brains right away. You send a certified or registered letter, return receipt, to the president, stating your case. Enclose a copy of the document you had given his marketing people. It should be dispassionate and businesslike, chief executive to chief executive, a matter of protecting your rights. Consummately firm, with a hint of more to come if need be.

You don't say it outright, but you subtly imply you will be willing to settle for a very decent fee rather than bring it to litigation. You, a small entrepreneur, are hardly in a position to engage in a drawn-out, costly, time-consuming, high-powered legal proceeding versus an industrial giant.

You check your letter with a lawyer friend to make sure it won't damage a legal case if it comes to that.

LETTER TO THE COMPANY PRESIDENT

September 23, 1993   BY CERTIFIED MAIL

Mr. C. Stevens McLaury
President
Bryant Distillers International, Ltd.

_____
_____

Dear Mr. McLaury:

I saw something in the newspaper yesterday that left me very much disturbed. It should disturb you, too. It touches at the heart of how we make a living here at our company.

Let me explain:

On December 12, 1992, eight months ago, we made a presentation of a new concept—unique, never done before—to get a market-share lift of your top-selling vodka brand. And, here's the brilliance of the idea—to have the market share continue to rise perceptibly, long range. In other words, this was a plan to switch consumers of a competitive brand of vodka to your brand and to maintain the loyalty of a significant percentage of these new customers.

We had an eighty-page document for implementing this project, which included trade and consumer advertising plus direct mail and telemarketing. Two copies were left with your executives at the meeting. Quite a package. They told us without reservation that they liked and admired our idea very much.

I saw our concept in a magazine ad yesterday, in full bloom. Or something so close to our basic idea and its implementation that you'll be hard put to distinguish between the two. It's being run by your regular agency, not by us.

As I noted before, marketing ideas are our business. We get paid for them. That's how we make a living. We've been doing fine because we are creative as well as good businesspeople who know how to hit the jugular of consumer persuasion.

I'm sure you will be fair. We will be, too.

We're looking forward to hearing from you shortly.

                                             Very truly yours,

Put a Rival Idea to Rest. Kill It After Your Client Examined It.

Two letters:

Slash and burn.

Less painful demise.

Situation: You are an account executive at a marketing services company. Your major assignment is a medical equipment manufacturer, which represents a big slice of your company's revenue. A firm that specializes in telemarketing presented a sales development plan to your client that was quite ingenious. It is a marketing thrust that uses telemarketing, direct mail, and advertising, all working together. It has the stamp of the popular buzzword, integrated marketing, which interests your client. Their marketing director asked you to critique it.

Strategy: You have to kill this proposal by an interloper who threatens your coveted client relationship. Who needs a rival in your rosy picture? This can start as a benign irritation and eventually become a malignant cancer.

You can handle it in either of two ways. Kill it with a heavy stroke, or give it a more humane execution.

A letter is shown for each of these approaches.

THE SLASH AND BURN VERSION

March 16, 1993

Ms. Millicent Howard
Vice President, Corporate Communications
Saphire Medical Diagnostics

_____

_____

Re: Topline Report on the MacAdoo Plan

Dear Millicent:

The plan that MacAdoo Marketing Co. presented to you is moving along nicely: off the edge of the desk and into the trash heap.

I'm glad you asked us to check this out thoroughly and give our comments. This plan sounded glamorous at first glance, but it didn't measure up under thorough investigation.

Believe me, we scrutinized it rigorously with the aim of making it operational. But there were potholes that couldn't be paved over without spending more money than the project could bring to the bottom line. We detailed all this and will send along a full report this week.

I hate to be thumbs-down on this. Our normal instincts are to build on an idea and make it work. But in this case, there weren't enough redeeming features to offset the negatives. Briefly, MacAdoo should stick to telemarketing alone, which is what they are in business for.

We're working to develop a program that will achieve your objectives. We're poring over it from the bottom up to make sure it will work great. We'll be ready to review this with you in about thirty days. I'm confident you and your top management will go for it all the way.

Regards,

March 16, 1993

Ms. Millicent Howard
Vice President, Corporate Communications
Saphire Medical Diagnostics

_____

_____

Re: Topline Report on the MacAdoo Plan

Dear Millicent:

It was good you asked us to put a fine-tooth comb to MacAdoo's proposal. It's an innovative idea, and will probably get you a lot of publicity. Our instincts might say, let's go . . . at first look, but it comes apart under careful scrutiny.

The MacAdoo shop is loaded with professional skill in telemarketing, one of the best in this industry. I wouldn't hesitate to use them for a major phone project.

But MacAdoo fell down in developing an overall marketing plan that includes advertising, direct mail, and incorporates telemarketing as one of its elements. In my opinion, they should stick to their knitting.

They were good at setting up the rationale. Their concept was good. The presentation was good. But their proposal didn't address some practical realities—minefields where the whole vehicle will blow up.

In other words, what MacAdoo did was almost good. But the word "almost" spells the difference between smash winner and sorry loser. They said you would get a lot of publicity, but who wants publicity for a failure?

I think we owe MacAdoo some thanks for their commendable effort. Let's keep them in mind when telemarketing expertise is needed.

A full report will be delivered to you next week.

Regards,

P.S.   We are working on a plan to do what you want and then some. We're going over it carefully to get rid of some bugs. It will be doable, profitable, and objective-oriented. In fact, it will be great. We'll be ready to show it to you in thirty days.

An Associate Is Hacking at Your Proposal. Undo the Damage.

Situation: Your big idea on which you made a written presentation was virtually demolished by the critical memo of an associate at your company. It really centered on details rather than substance. His caustic comments are putting it to rest even though you believe the idea has excellent merit.

You know he is engaging his highly developed political-infighting skills to put you down, which is a good clue that your proposal is exceptional. You have to undo the damage, get your proposal on line, and repair your reputation.

Strategy: Tell the criticizer in a memo, with copies to the other execs, that his concern lies with operational details, not the idea itself, which has eminent merit. He shouldn't nitpick a good idea to death.

You created an innovative business enhancement concept. There was no need for operational purity at this juncture. That comes later.

Play on the criticizer's ego—his amazing gift of recognizing a good concept and the ability to make it work. Enlist the cooperation of your colleagues, including the criticizer, to work out the operation and get this brainchild on the road.

Tell them that it warrants everyone pitching in. It's for the good of the company. Say that putting this idea to work will bring the company industry-wide acclaim, which will rub off on everyone involved in it.

This is the way to get your plan on the front burner. When the operational procedures are ironed out, you will write up the program in its final form, under your name, and take charge. Let's face it. You originated the idea and deserve the glory.

IN-HOUSE MEMO

March 15, 1994

To: Bob Travis

From: Peggy Wallenberg

c.c. Zoe Callaway
Mel Hirsch
Elena Munoz

IN EXTREMIS—In the last extreme, next to death.

I'm sure this is not what you intended. But in effect, this is what your comments could conceivably cause to happen to the real estate investment plan my group put together.

This was a preliminary proposal. Its intent was to lay out the big picture; there was no time to button down all the details. Look on it as a vector to corporate income growth. I'm sure you didn't mean to kill it because of the unique gift you have of building on an essentially good idea, not discarding it. You do this exceedingly well.

Others who have read the proposal think the idea is intriguing and has great merit. We all realize, of course, that there are some rough edges to be smoothed out. Indeed, your comments confirmed this, and at the same time they were helpful in indicating how this can be made into a very vital program.

Let's all meet on Thursday to discuss the implementation of this plan, one that will enable us to enhance our company's net worth. We now have the head and body in place, all we need is the bloodstream to give it life. It all boils down to our determination to make a good thing work.

My group will then prepare a final plan based on everyone's input, which will include the operational methodology and a timing schedule for the introduction. We'll then be ready for an early spring start.

This will be a big coup for all of us, on which we all deserve credit—and the praise when it's introduced.

Regards,

Peggy

Company Politics Obliges You to Endorse an Idea to Your Client, but You Don't Want Them to Accept It.

Situation: You are an account executive at a company that acts as a sales broker for various record labels. An important account you handle is number two in pop music records. A senior executive in your company has an idea for promoting their new releases through a venue they had never used before—the loudspeakers at racetracks and betting parlors.

First of all, it's not good to have ideas for your client coming from anyone but you. It dilutes your importance on the account.

Secondly, you particularly don't like it coming from this guy, who is trying to wheedle his way into being your supervisor on this piece of business. Initiating an innovative idea is a good way for him to start.

Thirdly, the idea doesn't fit your client's customer profile. Indeed, his idea is lousy, and you would look bad if you approved of it.

Strategy: Ask the senior executive to give his recommendation to you in a memo. Send a copy of the memo to your client, with a covering letter. Your letter can't appear negative because the senior guy expects you to support him, and you are obliged to do so. But you do not necessarily want to show that you, in truth, agree with it.

Bottom line: You don't want your client to accept this idea, but you have to appear gung ho loyal within your company.

You will meet with your client later and give him a more pointed oral opinion.

LETTER TO YOUR CLIENT

October 27, 1993

Mr. Sheldon Kaplan
Vice President
Dynamo Records Corporation

_____

_____

Dear Shelly:

One of our senior people here, Dick Rogers, has an idea for hyping some of your new releases that he thinks you should consider. A good idea can come from any source, which is why I don't hold back on putting it in front of you. Dick explained his idea in a memo to me, which I'm attaching.

Please don't brush it off strictly because it may not be consistent with the marketing plan we formulated. The audience he suggests we promote may be out of kilter with your target consumers, which we pointed out to Dick. So think of this, if you will, from the viewpoint of broadening your customer base, which is a noteworthy point.

Please hold off on any negative opinions you may have until I talk to you about it when we meet this coming Thursday.

Regards,

Protect Your Ideas from Being Neutered by Corporate Inertia.

Situation: You were recently hired for a top spot, exec VP, director of planning, at a giant retailer. Their image and sales have been slipping the past couple of years, gradually being outdistanced by smart, hungry competitors.

The chairman and CEO saw you several times before you got this coveted brass ring. You obviously impressed him, and he put his blessing on you, pushing your name to the top of the list. It's apparent they wanted a quarterback who could turn the game around. Your reputation is that of a catalyst who gets things done in a hurry.

After looking at all the plays and players, you are convinced you can come up with the game plan that gets the company out of its slump and start winning.

Your first presentation on how to go about building the business is scheduled for review by a new Project Growth Committee. You clearly sense opposition because the ground-breaking concepts you will display are antithetical to the corporate psyche of the committee members. Their resistance to your initiatives is clearly imminent.

Strategy: Send a pre-presentation letter to the chairman, who will not be at the presentation session, preparing him for negativism by the committee. Serve notice that the ingrained attitude of fear of the new retards progress, prevents ground-gaining offensives, and keeps the company in its dormant state and on a slow road to oblivion.

You assume you were hired to turn things around, but it can't happen with the stodgy attitude you fear will choke the life out of the plans you will be presenting.

LETTER TO THE CHAIRMAN

November 15, 1993

To: Ms. Loretta Springfield
        Chairman and CEO
        Sherwood & Company, Inc.

From: Steven Danouski

This letter will only take two minutes. It's an important two minutes.

I'm scheduled to deliver my new-horizons presentation to the Project Growth Committee next Friday. It's my first real performance here since I came on the scene. I just want to make a few private pre-presentation comments to you.

I notice a resistance here to new thinking that does not conform with the way things have been done. In effect, it is a resistance to new ideas that seem to upset tradition. I know you agree that we should not stay within a well-worn, narrow decision-making path.

"We can't do it here" is what I've heard so regrettably often in the short time I've been around. We both know it stifles progress. Progress in building income and net worth, which is what I was hired for.

Some of the ideas I'm going to present are new marketing concepts that will give us a competitive advantage and increase our sales volume. One is structured to improve our image and our customer franchises rather than see our image continue to decline. Another will recommend that we abandon properties and projects that are losers.

My presentation should be given serious consideration on its creativity and its merits rather than its adherence to corporate folklore. Each of the ideas should be looked upon as to how it can be made operative—the sooner the better. We have to dispense with the "it's not right for us" syndrome. I know you agree and will have an open mind on my proposals.

I'll finish up my two minutes with this Oscar Wilde quote, which I know reflects your own thinking: "Conformity is the refuge of the unimaginative."

Best wishes,

Steven Danouski

Power, Prestige . . . Protect, Build, Strengthen Your Image.

Counterattack a Shark Who Tried to Chew You Up.

Situation: You are a VP and account executive at a large advertising agency. A big-name executive had been forced to resign from another agency, and your president took him off the beach and hired him as a senior VP. His immediate duties are less than his position and salary can rationalize. Part of his activity is as an adviser on various corporate problems that come up.

He roams about looking for opportunities to enhance his presence and take over important responsibilities. He targeted you and delivered an Uzi assault-rifle blast, seizing on a plan you are about to present to your client. He derided it as fatuous and pedestrian and said that it could even lose this account. This was in a memo to you with copies to the president and other key executives. His all-out attack shows his confidence in being able to replace you on this business, using this issue as a lever.

You know the account you handle is in good shape, and the customer likes you. You also know your plan is good. It's well done, and your client already knows the guts of it and is pleased. Mr. Shark obviously didn't check the background of this plan or the account.

Two strategies:

I. Come out swinging. A no-holds-barred knockout punch.

II. Sharp counterattack. Box and jab with confidence. A knock-out now, or perhaps in round two.

Strategy I: You hurry to see the president to inquire about this sudden and unwarranted outpouring of venomous criticism. You take the position that aside from being wrong, it's highly insulting and not good for the business.

The president is clearly simpatico with you. He knows you are on solid ground with this account. They are happy with you and the agency. Your plan is virtually accepted. It would be nuts to rock the boat.

The president doesn't like this guy anyway. He knows he is getting too bold and disruptive. He gives you carte blanche to go to it. You decide to come out swinging and go for a one-round knockout.

Strategy II: A firm, unequivocal, yet slightly tempered counterattack. You have the ammunition to go for the kill, but you use businesslike restraint. Sarcasm is in order. You are readying yourself to throw the knockout punch if it goes another round.

April 26, 1994

To: Harrison C. Rommer

From: Carlo DeLuria

c.c.   Harry Adams   John Garfield, President
        Ginny Carpenter
        Bernie Fogel
        Seth Gordon

> "It is much easier to be critical than to be correct."
> (Benjamin Disraeli)

I sure didn't expect your crushing criticism of my Augustine plan. WOW! A copy was sent to you as a courtesy, but you certainly didn't show any when you summarily blasted off a castigating memo to me.

First of all, you don't know the background of this account. The plan hits the bull's-eye of Augustine's objectives beautifully. It's thoughtfully conceived, gets to the heart of the problem, and is skillfully written.

Secondly, this account is being very well run at our company. Their sales are strong; they are happy. We're doing an excellent job for them. It's nicely profitable for us.

In the third place, don't you think you should have spoken to me before dashing off this abusive and personally insulting diatribe? With copies to top executives of this company, including the president?

I'll quote another piece of advice by Disraeli, that legendary politician par excellence:

> "To be conscious that you are ignorant is a great step to knowledge."

Truly yours,

Carlo De Luria

SHARP COUNTERATTACK

April 26, 1994

To: Harrison C. Rommer

From: Carlo DeLuria

c.c.   Harry Adams   John Garfield, President
        Ginny Carpenter
        Bernie Fogel
        Seth Gordon

> "It is much easier to be critical than to be correct."
> (Benjamin Disraeli)

This quote is an understatement in commenting on your memo about my Augustine plan, sent to me and all of the above without warning. I appreciate your comments, since it shows a view that an outside person could have—without knowing the facts.

Without giving you all the facts, which will take several pages and which you can look up in the files, I'll mention these particularly salient points.

First, the client has a certain objective that this plan targets right in the center of the bull's-eye. It gets to the heart of what they want done with a skillfully conceived, well-documented operational design. It embodies good thinking on the part of the agency staff.

Secondly, this account is being very well run here. Our campaigns are successful. The client is happy. The agency is happy. It generates good income for us.

Harrison, I wish you had come to me before sending your memo. It might have been good to talk it over so I could have had the benefit of your comments beforehand and been able to explain the fallacy of your criticism.

And it wouldn't have needlessly created a cause célèbre by bringing in all the other people you c.c.'d. It even might have been helpful, certainly more businesslike. Let's do it this way next time.

Truly yours,

Carlo De Luria

Eliminate an Unwanted Heir to Your Job Slated to Dispossess You.

Situation: A leading White House staffer once said, ''Politics is a contact sport.'' This is true as well in the executive suite of TGF Broadcasting Network, where you are the majordomo of sales. You've been ensconced there for eighteen years, credited with billions in sales over this time, an often-quoted leader in the industry. Just the same, your slip is showing. Sales slip, that is. Down 14 percent.

TGF's chief of chiefs thinks you've had it, and rumors waft about that he wants you eased out. He picked a young Doberman with sharp teeth, a loud-mouth sales ace from a rival network, to come in and work under you. Of course, you met with the newcomer in advance of hiring and approved.

Approved? There was little choice the way he was bequeathed to you. ''After all, Jerry, you should be very happy to get this kind of help. Why should you be working day and night? We had a hard time getting this guy and had to pay a lot to move him. We did it just for you.''

It doesn't make sense for a hotshot at this newcomer's level to be your assistant. You see the chief's grand plan starting to go into action. Doberman will be an undercover agent, there to learn what is needed to inveigle his way into your fold and make you redundant; then you will be delicately eased out to well-deserved pastureland.

Strategy: You are not ready for it. You will not be jostled up and out this way. You wholeheartedly welcome your heir-to-be and start his initiation toward becoming a marvelous asset—eventually, perhaps, as good as you are.

But first, he must get a grounding on the station affiliate setup. It stands to reason that he must acquire expertise on the network before he can sell it. You assign him to this essential undertaking and tell him to write a report on how to improve whatever needs improving.

Likewise, he must gather intelligence on the future plans of the rival networks and report his analysis of their prospective ratings, prices, audiences, and so forth.

Give Doberman this schedule, so essential to his career at the network, in a letter to his home a few days before he steps into the office.

These assignments will take months and require lots of travel, making him almost invisible on the executive floor. Further, the reports are bound to be disasters. You, of course, will give him all the help possible. If he is discredited, you are blameless. This network demands the most talented and brilliant.

LETTER TO YOUR "HEIR"

April 18, 1994

Mr. Harvey Duran
38 Heather Drive

_____

_____

Dear Harvey:

Great news for both of us! I'll have the widest open arms to welcome you here at TGF Broadcasting.

As Chuck told you, you'll be reporting to me, and I sure need your help. Indeed, I'll be looking to you to take over a big part of my duties so that I'll be able to move on to other things that I can't talk about now.

I know, Harvey, that you want to get a close hold on sales as soon as possible. However, I'd first like you to take hold of a couple of other very important operations that need doing. In addition to helping us out tremendously at this time, it will give you a good foundation of knowledge that will be extremely essential when you get into the thick of sales.

1. Get to know our major affiliate stations. Find out their gripes, their hopes, what they like about us and how they think we can improve. I've covered this with Jim Erhart, in charge of affiliate relations, and he's all for it. By the same token, sit with the managers of our owned-and-operated stations.

    Then write a complete report of what you found out, your analysis, and conclusions. This will be extremely valuable, as I'm sure you clearly see. This is a wonderful opportunity for you to learn our station lineup and become an expert on the network. Frankly, the people here can't wait to see your report.

2. When the above report is finished, carry out surveillance of what our competition will be doing this fall, particularly daytime programming. In your own inestimable way, as I've been told, try to get a fix on the ratings they anticipate and how likely they are to make it happen. Cable, of course, has to be part of the picture.

    Naturally, this will have to be a product of your expert reasoning and intuition based on the intelligence you gather. I don't have to tell you how important this will be when we get into the major selling season.

These are tall missions, Harvey, and so important in getting our sales pitch in excellent shape. We're all depending on you. Don't forget, I'll be the first one to lend a hand if you need any help. Just give me a holler.

I have a whole orientation and greeting procedure lined up for you right from the starting whistle: lunches, cocktail meetings, and so on. See me as soon as you step in the door.

I won't say the best of luck, because I know you'll make your luck. We all know you'll do great.

Jerry Sullivan

A High-Visibility Project That You Devised Turned Out to Be a Bust. Avoid the Blame. Maintain Your High Standing.

Situation: You are the dynamo head of marketing at a long-distance phone company. You engineered a joint promotional venture with a famous packaged-goods–baked goods marketer, Happy Bakers, for their popular cake and cookie brands.

    Getting in bed with this huge consumer franchise looked like a marvelous coup. You proudly pulled it off. Your company's brass were excited. People shook your hand as you strutted around the office.

    You assigned the program's operation to one of your managers, Jason Miller, who had been proven reliable and conscientious in carrying out his assignments.

    The promotion flopped. The latest hot-line data from the field confirmed the bad news. The consumer offer was not good, and Happy Bakers' consumer characteristics do not coincide with your customer profile. Jason pointed this out right away but was quickly overruled. He bowed to your wishes and took charge of the promotion as a good soldier should.

    Jason is willing to take the stigma of blame for this fiasco in order to protect you. He figures you will then owe him a favor to be bestowed at some future time.

Strategy: Send a memo about the baleful news of the promotion to the chief executive officer and the chief operating officer.

    Downplay the downside. Emphasize an upside. Avoid being beholden to Jason Miller while indicating him to be blameworthy.

September 10, 1993

Mr. Roger Sears, President & CEO
Speedvoice, Inc.

_____

_____

Re: The Happy Bakers Tie-in

cc: Carlos Podesta, COO

Dear Mr. Sears:

I just got our new hot-line report from the field on our Happy Bakers joint promotion.

Surprisingly, it doesn't demonstrate any renewed life to the point where it can be
profitable for us to continue. The two market tests showed good promise, so it's
hard to account for this. It's too soon to determine why it didn't work on the rollout.
We all thought it would be great, including everyone at headquarters.

I recommend aborting it now. We will then analyze the figures and find out how
the promotion was carried out and whether the problem is conceptual, systemic, or
whatever.

Fortunately, I decided to move this ahead gradually and also to put it into an
intensive care posture and monitor it every step of the way. So far, we went to only
30 percent of the country, so we caught the negatives early. And because we
watched our expenses carefully, there is no big loss. This caution certainly paid off.

The good news is that our excellent rapport with Happy Bakers is undiminished.
They will still do joint promotions with us, which could involve any one or more
of their incredible brand franchises.

In addition, we will be working on joint ventures with other class A companies.

As mentioned before, we'll look into why this one didn't measure up to what we all
expected. Thus, it will turn out to be a wonderful test for future promotions, which
is what we need.

Jason Miller, in my department, spearheaded the program. I selected him because
he had always been very reliable on other projects. He put the market test data
together, which gave us the green light. However, I held him back from making a
fast national rollout. I can't really fault Jason, since I obviously have to shoulder
the responsibility.

It's pretty difficult to bat 1,000. Our batting average is still very good, and there
are some great promotions in the pipeline. You'll be thrilled when you hear about
them.

Regards,

A Colleague's Proposal Undermined You. Kill It with High Praise.

Situation: You are a group product manager in a division of a large manufacturer of health-care equipment. A colleague wrote a product introduction plan for two products soon to be ready for launching. One is a product she is responsible for; the other is your product. She recommends that the same procedure is right for both and that doing them in tandem will save the company a load of money. She is willing to handle the duo introduction.

It makes sense, but isn't she trespassing on your turf? Taking the wind out of your sails with a highly visible, bold move? You were outmaneuvered. You feel awfully dumb.

The plan is competently documented and well written. It focuses on your colleague's brand, with adroit references to your product being a logical companion entry in the introductory launch.

Strategy: You can't condemn the plan. You have to enter your voice with the other management people in a common show of admiration, particularly since your brand is directly involved. *But this must not be allowed to continue.*

You decide to play a bureaucratic game by urging a series of meetings, reviews, assessments, profit analyses, more meetings, and so forth—supposedly with the ardent aim of getting the plan into play, but through a tortuous route of consummate marketing discipline, which will put it into the cesspool of inoperative brilliant initiatives.

Meanwhile, you will write your own plan for your product to be held in abeyance, ready to spring it when the timing is right.

IN-HOUSE MEMO

November 16, 1993

To: Heidi Sherwood
            Colin Burke
            Luisa Alvarez
            Kathy Marshall

From: Sheridan Johnson

Your market penetration plan is a great piece of work—and very well documented, especially in terms of ethnic and seasonal variables. And certainly well presented. Congratulations, Heidi. You must have worked on this a long time.

My unqualified vote is to put this on mainstream for further review and on the way to implementation. The initial aim, of course, is to get it to a market test as soon as possible.

Since my brand is involved, I suggest we all write down the factors to address in the next stage of decision making, including any inherent problems that must be addressed. As a start, here are my recommendations on what needs to be reviewed:

> What kind of market testing should we do before we roll out? How many cities, what information should we look for, etc.? Should we follow the procedure in the plan as written or try to get additional data before making a final decision?

> Does the profit projection for each product warrant the amount of investment that is recommended? How much do we actually save with a dual introduction when the extra sales department costs are considered?

> Will the detail men be confused? Will our trade accounts be confused as well?

> Will the impact of either or both products be diluted by launching them together?

> What effect will this have on doctors' prescriptions? Will they be confused?

I believe these questions have logical answers, but it's important they be addressed, since this is an introduction of two important products.

I would like to see this plan go. Let's all get behind it and make it work.

Sheridan Johnson

cc: Gerald Rosen, CEO
     The New Product Planning Committee

Give Comrade-in-Arms Support to Your Colleague's Plan, While Making Sure *Your* Plan Replaces It.

Situation: A fellow executive came up with an innovative plan for a new business acquisition process. It sounds great—on paper—and it could work. That is, if certain details are straightened out, if the operational procedure is put into place, and if it gets staff support.

   You want to make an end run around it with your own plan, which you have formulated in your mind but not yet put on paper. Why shouldn't you be the big player in an important business development program?

   You need time to develop your idea, which is why you have to stall your friend's plan. It has to be consigned to the "good but never will be" pile.

   You can't be negative. You want to seem supportive, a loyal team member. And, by all means you want to maintain your colleague's comradeship and be a strong arm by his side.

Strategy: Send a memo to your colleagues, with copies to the other executives involved and the COO, stating your enthusiastic endorsement. Say it's a function of perfecting the operational details in order to make it a winner. It will require thinking, meetings, and the delegation of responsibilities. You are gung ho, and you say the others should give their active support too.

   Actually, your colleague's plan could be trouble-free if sufficient time is spent in setting up the procedure. However, you have created a bureaucratic quagmire. In effect, your so-called enthusiastic endorsement has put this plan into a corporate dung heap.

IN-HOUSE MEMO TO THE COLLEAGUE

December 7, 1993

To: Tim Spiegel
Ambrose Adams
Laura Cohen
MacDonald Michaels
Mr. James E. Johnson, President

From: Allen Schroeder

Great work! Your proposal for realigning our new business development committee into an action-oriented department is innovative, and then some. It's a well-conceived, expertly prepared document, and it looks like it could be very effective. You have created a fine blueprint.

It would be good if we all hopped on board to iron out the procedures and make it work, keeping in mind the oft-quoted caveat: There's a devil in the details. I'm confident the details can be worked out if we all pitch in. This is too good to be allowed to sit by the wayside.

Tim, please get a task force together to get this moving. I believe this group should start by defining the purpose and the goals. I suggest they then set up a procedure for each facet of the operation, with the specific people designated for handling each step, even if more personnel have to be hired.

To show my enthusiasm in concrete terms, I'm volunteering my services to develop an outline of the steps that have to be taken. I want to do this even though it looks like I'll be extremely busy for the next few weeks.

Congratulations,

Allen Schroeder

Make an Ally out of a Rival. Form a Powerful Alliance.

Two strategies, two letters.

Situation: You are a group product manager at a packaged foods titan—bright, resourceful, glib, and ambitious. A few doors down the hall sits another group product manager. He is about your age and is also bright, resourceful, glib, and ambitious. The nature of the work environment, your personalities, and the air that permeates the halls manifests an unspoken rivalry between you. There is an underlying shuffle as you each try to outshine the other. The ceaseless bobbing and weaving, with an outward display of camaraderie, stresses both of you out.

You have decided that a comradely blending of talents and intelligence will make you each go farther faster. You can be a powerhouse team. There's plenty of room for two near the top. Once you both get there, the rivalry can commence for the jeweled scepter.

Strategy I: An opportunity comes up. You are both engaged in developing your product plans for the coming year. Each must follow the same outline guide, which includes a forecast of the total corporate growth pattern over the next five years.

It makes sense to have both plans show the same forecast figures. Having different data would reflect badly on both plans. There will be questions. Which one is correct? Why the difference? Why not get together to work on the corporate forecast? This is the conception of a powerful alliance.

Strategy II: You happen to be at a lull. Your rival is in a hectic overtime mode. Make an altruistic offer to help. Say you would be willing to work under him, as an assistant if need be, in order to get him over the hump.

This is a way to get a partnership started. A comradely do-what's-best-for-the-company gesture. You know the assistant role won't be taken seriously once you become involved. Again, this is the conception of a powerful alliance.

September 16, 1993

To: Jerry Hoppindale

From: JoAnn Raab

It doesn't make sense. What doesn't make sense, you might ask?

It doesn't make sense for me to work on a project in which I have to analyze and make forecasts on a set of data when you are working on another project that requires the same kind of forecasts on the same data. $2 + 2 = 8$—why not forecast together?

It's likely that our concerted effort will produce a more intelligent prognostication of the future growth of the company than each doing it solo. Importantly, two different forecasts will confuse management and they won't believe either one. It will be a lot less work for each of us. Finally, it is efficient and more effective.

As so well stated by Samuel Goldwyn, the summa cum laude movie tycoon: "Forecasts are dangerous, especially about the future."

Regards,

JoAnn Raab

September 16, 1993

To: Jerry Hoppindale

From: JoAnn Raab

I see you are snowed under right now with much to do and virtually impossible deadlines. I'll be in a relative lull for another couple of weeks because I have to wait for more product test results before I can start to develop my plans.

Why not let me help you get over the hump? It won't solve your entire problem, but another body working for you should ease it up a bit.

I'm not familiar with your products, but I'll take orders from you, just as if I'm one of your assistants. Jerry, I hate to say this, but this is not entirely unselfish. Your help would be more than welcome if I were in a similar spot and you could find the time to pitch in.

Regards,

JoAnn Raab

Shock and Disappointment on Arrival at a Big New Job. Your Office Is No Way Near What It Should Be.

Situation: You've been appointed as a senior executive at a bank holding company. You appeared at your new office and got a startling jolt, followed by shock. You wonder, is this the right place? The right address? Did they forget about your job title? Did you really get this job? Have I been had?

    Your office is certainly not what your title calls for. It's small. An inside location. And further, it's rather unkempt. Obviously, there's a mistake. Your ire reaches out to the whole company.

Strategy: Inform the office manager in writing, right away. There has to be an immediate change of location. However, you don't want to start off by throwing your weight around and demanding the proper trappings of your authority. You want your image to be that of a nice guy, of an officer with a feeling for the enlisted folks. You are aware of the current management principle that the best way to win loyalty and obedience is through love and admiration, not fear.

    Your message to the office manager must be firm but not overbearing. It must be insistent, yet with a light approach. Putting it in the form of a poem is a good touch. Make it whimsical, marking you from the beginning as a smart, creative, easy-to-get-along-with executive who knows what he wants—and knows he must get it.

IN-HOUSE MEMO
(TO BE WRITTEN TO THE OFFICE MANAGER
IN LONGHAND.)

November 17, 1993

To: Todd Franklin, may I record a complaint.
Proper and businesslike, with calm restraint.

An appeal to you, Todd, I ask for your pity.
No intent to amuse, or to seem smart or witty.

I'm bereft, bewildered, befuddled, bemused.
Feeling so weary, so wanting, so woefully abused.

Why hasn't it happened, what I should expect?
No window, no couch, nor even respect.

Should I leave quietly, go home for a week?
And when I return find in place what I seek?

Pardon the longhand, Todd, I have no secretary.
Please call me on 941, I'm not in the directory.

Seth Hamilton
Senior Vice President
Consumer Banking

You Are on Your Company's Board by Special Mandate. Tell Them Why You Are a First-Rate Choice.

Situation: You are a senior pilot at Global Airlines and were appointed a member of the board of directors. It came about because, after a hard fight with the pilots' union, it was agreed, among other things, that the union could have one seat on the board. You were the one chosen.

    The other board members perceive you as an incongruity that was forced on them.

Strategy: Send a formal message to the board members explaining why you are just as qualified as of any of them to be seated in the boardroom. And, in fact, you bring a meaningful perspective to the board that was previously lacking. You have a vital interest in the future of the airline, a deep knowledge of the company at all levels, and a good business sense as well, particularly as it pertains to flight operations. Be deferential but firm in stating this rationale.

LETTER TO THE CHAIRMAN OF THE BOARD

May 18, 1994

A Message to the Board of Directors of Global Airlines, Inc.
From Your Newest Member, Leon Harrison
Spencer Rosencrans, Chairman

_____   _____
_____   _____
_____   _____
_____   _____

I am honored to serve with you on the board of this company. I'm a senior pilot at Global, as you all know, and have worked here for twenty-five years.

I suppose you may consider me an incongruity, since my appointment is the result of a deal the pilots' union made with the company whereby we are to be represented on the board with one member. I'm the one that was selected.

As well as being an employee in a senior position, I'm also a stockholder, with a good part of my savings invested here. My interest, as is yours, is in having this company prosper. If it doesn't, I'm out of a job, as will be the case with the many thousands of other people who work here. Further, the funds for my retirement, consisting mostly of Global stock, will be devastated.

So you see, my future, the happiness of my family, and my kids' college education, all depend on it. All my thinking and all my efforts are for the whole company, not just the pilots, the maintenance people, the clerks, the executives, or any other group.

My training has been very specialized. All I do is fly passengers around the world. (Let's face it, isn't this the raison d'etre of this company?) But I also read a lot about the business functions—finance, marketing, legal, customer service, and so on. I'm immersed in it. And I intimately know the character and culture of Global.

What I also bring here are common sense, integrity, and loyalty to this enterprise. And a deep-seated yearning to have this company be vital and prosperous in this dog-eat-dog industry.

I am gratified to be joining you in helping to shape the destiny of Global Airlines.

Leon Harrison

Leon Harrison
Member of the
Board of Directors

Explain Your Demotion. Make It Look Like a Promotion.

Situation: You've been an employee of a food-processing company for twenty-six years, the past twelve as the national sales manager. You've been transferred, actually demoted, to special markets sales. It's kind of a backwater slot. A youthful executive was brought in to take your place, a matter of young blood replacing an old-timer.

    The company wants to keep you on because of the friendships you built up with customers. Everybody likes you. It would be bad customer relations to put you on the street. The company would seem grubby and heartless.

Strategy: Send a letter to the customer-friends you had been contacting for so many years. Describe your new position as an upward move. Management wants you to help them on the big picture—planning for the future. Your know-how and creativity will be indispensable for this assignment.

    Management must be satisfied with the way your letter is phrased. Check it out with them. Also, show the letter to your replacement with the notation that it has management approval.

LETTER TO ALL YOUR EX-CUSTOMERS

September 22, 1993

Mr. George T. Mitolokis
Vice President
Selective Food Wholesalers, Inc.

_____

_____

Dear George:

I want you to know this good news before you hear about it officially. My job here has been changed to a front office position. I'm moving from sales manager–national to sales manager–special markets planning.

Management and I agree that it will give me a chance to take a step back, take my mind off day-to-day pressures, and help them plan for the long term. It's a way of taking advantage of my knowledge and creative talents to help the company grow.

It's a big responsibility, and I'm delighted management saw fit to put me in this spot. I'm not happy that I won't see you regularly, but I'll certainly stay in touch. You can be sure I'll drop by when I'm in your area.

Steve Callahan is taking over as national sales manager, and I'll be working with him so that there will be a clean transfer of customer responsibilities. Steve is a great guy and knowledgeable in the business. I know you'll like him.

Thanks, George, for all you've done for me. It was wonderful doing business with you. Having you as a friend puts delicious icing on the cake.

                                        Best wishes,

"Turning Down" a Job Offer Before You Are Rejected. Maintain Your Dignity and Prestige.

Two strategies:

  I. You are presently employed.

  II. You are out of work.

Situation: A high-level marketing position is open at a big-name hotel chain. The search is well publicized with various contenders identified in the press. Your name was cited as being in the final round. You found out through leaks that you will not get the offer. It's going to someone else.

Strategy I: You are working for a hotel chain, and you wanted to switch to this new post, which would be a nice step up. Your company knows you are in the competition and wishes you well, since it's a good upward move they can't match.

    You want to avoid the stigma of losing out to someone else. It signifies, in a way, a failure to measure up, which deals a sharp blow to your image inside and outside your present workplace.

    Write a letter requesting that you not be considered, giving a plausible rationale. The letter should be suitable for distribution to your colleagues and the press, if need be.

Strategy II: You are out of work. You don't want the world to know you were an also-ran for this position. Send a letter withdrawing your name so that you don't bear the stigma of rejection.

    Make it appear that you are very busy with consulting assignments that must be completed, which precludes your taking on this responsibility at the present time. Leave yourself open for the possibility of a future opportunity with the company.

March 14, 1994

Mr. Johan Mashida
President
Sigma Hotels, Inc.

_____

_____

Dear Johan:

This may come as a surprise to you in view of the close discussions we've had over the past several weeks on the position of senior VP, marketing director. I understand from rumors that it's coming down to the wire and my name is on the front-runner list.

It is, therefore, important that I get this message to you quickly. I thought about it for the last few days, talked it over with my family and associates, and finally came to the difficult decision of asking you to withdraw my name.

There is much to do in my present position, including certain important projects I started that I am obligated to see through to completion. I thought more and more about this as we got into final discussions. In good conscience, I cannot now abandon my present responsibilities.

I am honored by your consideration of me. And I'm most pleased that we got to know each other, which I hope is the start of a lasting friendship.

Sincerely yours,

March 14, 1994

Mr. Johan Mashida
President
Sigma Hotels, Inc.

_____

_____

Dear Johan:

As I had mentioned in our discussions, I have been in the midst of an important consulting assignment that I hoped would be winding down by this time. However, it is still going strong. In addition, I was recently called on by a major hospitality franchiser, which could lead to another assignment.

I therefore ask that my name be withdrawn from consideration for the position we had been reviewing, since I am presently unable to assume this responsibility in good conscience.

I am honored by your consideration and am most pleased to have met with you and your colleagues. Let's stay in touch. I hope the future will open up another opportunity to work together.

Most sincerely,

Protect Your Flanks . . . Combat Threats *from Within Your Company.*

Damning with Praise. Your Plan Was Turned Down for Another's. Make a Comeback.

Situation: You are a computer engineer at a software company. For the past three months you have been working to develop a software program for medical diagnosis. It will greatly reduce the time for amassing and analyzing huge amounts of data from a large number of medical tests and present them in a gestalt image—an important advance with a sizable market potential.

Another engineer in your company produced a plan for the same purpose. Ipso facto, the two of you were competing.

Your rival got a thumbs-up. His plan won out over yours. You know it's not as good as what you were carefully developing. His report to management was more spectacular—literate, colorful, replete with blue-sky analyses, full of bells and whistles. You can see that the staginess covers up snags and faults, but management went for it. You can't fight it. Not now.

The winner is a marvelous politician, a supreme infighter. He's glib with the answers, fast on his feet, rattles off intricate data with aplomb. A master at inducing smiles and affirmative head-shaking.

Sidle off with your tail between your legs? *No.* Your plan is better. It's not yet history.

Strategy: You now enlist in your competitor's camp. Pitch in with enthusiasm. Offer to spearhead his project, under him. You will do the spadework—developing, testing, perfecting—and relieve the creator of the day-to-day pressures. You'll keep him apprised of everything, of course, but he can now lean back and keep his mind on the big picture—on the meetings, the marketing, and the hype.

Your offer will sound very good, since your rival really doesn't want to get involved in the humdrum details. You've given him an excellent alternative. He's sure to take it.

You know his plan will not work without certain critical adjustments. There will be problems of complaints and recalls, if and when it is introduced to consumers as is. At this point your compatriot will be in over his head in remedying these glitches.

This will be done in the development and testing stages, which you are hands-on in charge of. Inch by inch, the plan's virtues will be chiseled away. One small error at a time will be uncovered by the careful, tedious testing you will be putting it through. Doubt after doubt will be revealed.

And, finally, it will have to be deservedly abandoned. Your friend's bluster will then look silly, his jokes no longer funny.

Then, your plan goes into operation. You will be working on the side, honing it, improving it, perfecting it. It will be ready on time as a replacement.

A smoke-screen maneuver? Yes, for a good purpose. You will have performed an exceptionally valuable service for your company.

IN-HOUSE MEMO TO THE WINNER

April 28, 1994

To: Lawrence Aldrich

From: Sam Berger
        Dick Devoe
        Meg Quinn
        Nimmo Kanaga

Re: Pitching In to Help on Your Trilateral Project

Let's get started now. This is too good to hold up even for a day. Here's my suggestions for getting your project to completion in the least amount of time:

I will take it upon myself to be the point man, reporting to you. We can have Meg handle the beta, and Nimmo the gamma components, and start producing them.

After there is enough to work with, even if it's not in finished form, we can start the testing of components. This should be done concurrently with the production, which will save a good three months in coming up with a marketable product.

There will be a final testing stage when production is completed to make sure there are no bugs before bringing this new software to market.

We have to give it a sexy name. It's up to you because you have such a good feel for what will grab the public.

This will give you the time you need for evaluating the reports and planning each step. You can handle the big picture without being diverted by day-to-day details. You will, of course, know everything that goes on every step of the way.

Best ever,

Sam

Make the Best of an Unhappy Situation. You Lost Out on a Pitch for a Major Account.

Four letters and memos that cover this regrettable episode.

Situation: You are the new business impresario at an advertising agency. You just got word that you came a close second in a six-agency scuffle for a much-coveted electronics account. There is very little comfort in losing; a close second might as well have been twenty-second.

Strategy Scenario: *Memo to you from your CEO*

He asks how come we didn't win, since we are a big-league agency and put so much time and money into this proposal.

Your memo to the CEO of your company and the troops

You want to express whatever positives can be squeezed out and help alleviate the pain of your position. There's hope for the future—not all is lost. Your presentation was very impressive and admired, even though you didn't win. Your pitch to this prospect hasn't stopped. There's still hope for winning some business from them.

The President sends a letter to the head of the winning agency

Congratulations. The best man won. (That is, the best presentation.)

The CEO sends a letter to the COO of the company they pitched

He wants to say that the COO made a good choice in the agency they selected. They are good, but so are we. But apparently not good enough in this encounter. He admires the way the COO is running his company and is impressed with his executives. Now that they got to know each other, he doesn't want to let the relationship lapse.

It took a lot of money and hard work to establish this contact. It would be very foolish not to build on it. You never know; it might pay off later.

MEMO TO YOU FROM YOUR CEO

March 10, 1994

To: Brian Goldsmith (Senior VP, Fuller Advertising, Inc.)

From: Jim Domaster (CEO, Fuller Advertising)

Well, we didn't get the DPI account, and I'll have to say we were all taken aback by the news. I'm disappointed, because your team put so much time and personnel into this presentation, not to say expense.

It's especially hard to take because we're better than Harris & Beeman, the winner over all the six agencies competing.

Was it the quality of the presentation? The way it was pitched? Our demeanor? Personalities? Inside politics? A bias towards the winning agency? What was it?

Let's analyze it for the future to make sure we get the maximum strength and advantage on the next new business presentation.

You have to keep pitching on DPI. It still has potential for business. And don't forget, we're the best ad agency in the business. And you are one of the folks here who makes us this way.

You mentioned that you and your people did your best.

We're not paid to do our best. . . . We're paid to win!

Jim Domaster

YOUR MEMO TO THE CEO OF YOUR COMPANY AND THE TROOPS

March 11, 1994

To: Jim Domaster, CEO

From: Brian Goldsmith

Copies: Sandi Solomon
         Bob Milkowski
         Serena Nukarab

We're now rising from the ashes after the DPI shoot-out. We came out second among the six agencies competing—actually, a very close second. I got this from the people I spoke with at DPI.

But second doesn't mean anything. It's like an election; either you win, or you lose. Winner takes all.

That's for now. Let's look to the future on this account. We made a good solid presentation with innovative ideas. It was eminently professional. Some of their people said it was very admirable. We gained a lot of respect for Fuller Advertising.

We also made some friends at DPI. We'll keep up these contacts. We have a big size-12 foot in the door. DPI has other business they could give us. And who knows what will happen on this business in six months or a year?

We'll take advantage of this valuable "in." It will pay off.

Brian Goldsmith

THE CEO'S LETTER TO THE HEAD OF
THE WINNING AGENCY

March 11, 1994

Mr. Emmon Beeman
President & CEO
Harris & Beeman

_____

_____

Dear Emmon:

It is with personal sadness and envy that I congratulate you on winning the DPI account.

Your shop made a stunning presentation. We were great, but you were superb.

I know you'll do a marvelous job on this business, and I wish you the best of luck.

How about getting together for a drink? I'd like to toast your well-deserved good fortune in person.

Best ever,

Jim Domaster

Jim Domaster
Chief Executive Officer
Fuller Advertising, Inc.

THE CEO'S LETTER TO THE COO OF THE COMPANY
THEY PITCHED

March 11, 1994

Mr. Milton D. Loquester
President & Chief Operating Officer
Data Processing International, Inc.

_____

_____

Dear Mr. Loquester:

You picked an excellent agency. We wish it were us, because we're excellent too, but obviously our presentation wasn't quite up to their level in this case.

In making this presentation, we got to know your people very well. We greatly admire them and their cooperation in giving us a fair shot.

I should also say that in our business we have contacts with a great many companies, and we're so impressed with the way you run yours. It is par excellence in every way. Naturally, everything we learned about DPI will remain confidential.

Now that we've gotten to know each other, let's not have our acquaintanceship lapse. I trust I can call you for advice from time to time. Likewise, I'm at your disposal.

Best regards,

Jim Domaster

Jim Domaster
Chief Executive Officer
Fuller Advertising, Inc.

You Must Justify Your Department's Existence to New Management.

Situation: Your company was taken over by a financial consortium. You now have new bosses, eager to quickly increase profits. They walked in with the attitude that efficiency must now rule, or they won't get their investment back. They seized on the perception that there are too many bodies around. So there was cut, cut—and likely more to come.

   They ask you, the manager of procurement, to tell them what your department does, your personal duties, what each of your staff does, and what efficiencies can be made. Your staff has already been reduced from eight to six because of the cutting frenzy.

Strategy: You decide to send them a narrative piece specifying the theory of procurement, your department's place in the company, and the extraordinary importance of what it does. You must emphasize procurement's crucial involvement in the whole business. Without you, everything ceases.

   You note that you and your people are overworked to the limit of endurance, but you perform gladly with pride. Essentially, you want to avoid losing any more of your people and to get the new overseers off your back.

IN-HOUSE MEMO TO THE HEAD OF THE RESTRUCTURING COMMITTEE

October 6, 1993

To: The Management Committee on Resource Usage
        J. Edgar Sawman, Chairman

From: Richard C. Donovan
        Director of Procurement

Subject: The Procurement Department—
         Our Mission and Structure

What We Do

Ordering supplies, equipment, and materials, and distributing them to the people at our plants is a simple, straightforward way of describing our task.

However, it doesn't seem simple when you consider that our responsibility is enormous. We obtain the goods that make this whole company run. If we don't do it economically—and with expert precision—everything will stop dead in the water.

Who Does It?

The staff personnel reporting to me has been downsized to five buyers and one information technician. We are now three fourths of our former staff. We've been reduced, restructured, programmed, and deprogrammed, and we came out of it with undiminished dedication to doing the best possible job. Sure, doing it with blood, sweat, and tears, but with a ferocious spirit of achievement because we want to help make this company prosper.

The Parts of Our Mission

Our personnel responsibilities consist of three basic functions. Each is MOST IMPORTANT.

1. KEEP THE ROUTINE ORDERING AND TRAFFICKING FLOWING WITHOUT A HITCH. Getting everything our plants and offices want, no matter how near or far. Getting it on time, in good condition, with the best quality for the purpose at the lowest price. Whew!

   Every executive, each and everyone in the whole company, sees this going on . . . every single day—like clockwork.

The next two functions are behind the scenes. You don't see them taking place.

2. SUPPLIER RELATIONS. We must make sure we have the best vendors. Their production capabilities, their shipping facilities, their financial strength, and much more all have to be checked and rechecked. This is to assure an efficient, on time, and reliable supply stream.

3. Now for the glamour part—NEW VISTAS. It's crucial that we keep up with

new technology, new ways to improve quality, increase efficiency, save money, and get ahead of the trend and the competition. All of this is little noticed until a new system gets put in the works for all to see.

As mentioned before, people and space have been cut here. We're lean, to the point of skinny, but not malnourished. We're mean, to the point of cruel, but sympathetic to everyone's needs. Very often we work without any thought of hours or weekends. We do it with enthusiasm and pride.

Think about it. What we do impacts on everything that takes place here. We deliver the goods that make this company run.

Respectfully submitted,

Richard C. Donovan

Richard C. Donovan

Survive a Corporate Downsizing.

Situation: You are a midlevel customer service manager at a field office of a world-renowned computer company. They are undergoing a severe downsizing. Rumors are running wild throughout the company about who is marked for termination and who survives. Everyone from the bottom up is scared. The underground company semaphore is signaling that your job is destined for the discard heap.

Strategy: You decide you can't just sit there defenseless with your neck on the guillotine block. You need your job, and you will exert every possible means to survive the upcoming carnage.

    The first act of preservation is to send a seemingly routine letter to the headquarters executive in charge of the downsizing, with a copy to the human resources chief, informing them of your work activities. You emphasize that on your own initiative you go far beyond your job description, which manifestly enhances your value manyfold.

    You have excellent rapport with major customers in your area. In addition to keeping them happy, you advise them on peripherals, software, and equipment upgrading, which leads to extra sales.

    In fact, considering your effectiveness in generating new business, you request that part of your workweek be officially allocated to the sales department. Make yourself seem as indispensable as possible.

    You've done the best you can to avoid being an unemployment statistic.

LETTER TO YOUR HEADQUARTERS MANAGEMENT

September 21, 1993

Mr. Clemson G. Acheson
Executive Vice President
Majestic Computers, Inc.

_____

_____

cc: Ms. Gwendolyn Hartnett Ritchie
      Vice President, Human Resources

Re: My Current Job Duties as Assistant Customer Service Manager—Houston Office

For management review, this will update you about my present work activity in the Houston office. As you will see, what I'm doing goes far beyond my prescribed duties.

Naturally, I fulfill all my responsibilities in handling service requests and complaints. However, I also put a big effort into predicting customer problems and heading them off as well as advising them about upgrades, peripherals, and software.

In so doing, I have developed a personal relationship with several of our more important customers. They often call me for guidance on utilizing their hardware more effectively and for equipment they may need.

When there is a lull, I visit customers to chat with them eye-to-eye. This is the best way to find out the technical details of our customers' programs and to advise them on using our equipment more efficiently. This has led to a large volume of sales we would not have otherwise obtained.

I'm convinced that my contribution to the company would be even further enhanced if part of my time were officially registered to the sales department. I could carry out this assignment concurrently with my customer service duties.

I believe this brings you up-to-date on my activities. Thank you so much for the opportunity to review this with you.

Very truly yours,

Otto C. Rickhoffer

Otto G. Rickhoffer
Assistant Customer Service
Manager, Houston Office

Deep Disappointment After You Merged Your Firm into a Larger Operation. Knotty Problems. Correct Them Quickly.

Situation: You are a respected attorney and the owner of a moderate-size law firm. After thirty-six years of building and nurturing it to its present highly reputable and profitable state, you decide to take it easy. The wisest course is to merge into a larger firm with plenty of personnel and facilities to handle your needs.

You will continue to take care of your clients but be relieved of most of the details and management travails. Your personal income is in relation to the income you generate. This was the plan when you spoke at length with the owners of the firm who succeeded in luring you.

Your business was much in demand. You had been courted by many medium and large law firms. The final winner pushed the right button to get you to zero in on them.

Two months have gone by, and you are worse off than before. There is lip service to your needs, nothing else. You are working harder and longer, with mounting pressure. And you are falling farther and farther behind.

Bottom line: You are disheartened. It's not working out. The owner-partners are sincere, but they neglect to personally mount a resolute effort to make it work for you.

The partners know they made a great deal in acquiring you. They have already spent several hundreds of thousands on this deal. They don't want to rock the boat. Having you undo what's been done would be very sorry news for them—unthinkable, in fact.

Strategy: You have leverage. You know the partners don't want to lose you. The wedding is over, but the courting has to continue. If you hint at dissolution, they will get panicky.

It won't take a lot to please you, but they have to roll up their sleeves and take charge and give the necessary orders to their staff. They have to sign the requisitions for the needed personnel and equipment.

You are meeting with them tomorrow to go over the matter of "How is it going?" You send them a memo today—a day in advance of your meeting—to specify your grievances and throw the problem in their laps. They have advance notice and can start thinking about what has to be done.

Give them a week to rectify your situation.

IN-HOUSE MEMO TO THE PARTNERS

April 7, 1994

Podesta, Saul, Weiner P.C.
> Tomasa Podesta
> Harry Saul
> John Podesta
> Steve Weiner

From: Sheila Epps

> In Advance of Our Meeting
> Tomorrow . . . Matters to Be
> Covered.
> Small Things Can Make for
> Big Problems If They're Not
> Taken Care Of.

In the spirit of doing what's best for the entire firm, and so that we all get maximum income and continued growth from the accounts I brought in, a number of adjustments have to be made.

These adjustments will relieve me of a great deal of anxiety, frustration, pressure, and unnecessarily long hours. And I should add, dissatisfaction and disaffection.

These are small things, really. All told, it doesn't amount to a great deal of expense. But only you can get it done, not me.

— My phone is chaotic. I don't have someone to answer my phone promptly and correctly or to take clear, knowledgeable messages.

— My phone is not equipped with one-touch dialing or memory. I can't continue to punch fourteen digits to make a call. I should have push-button memory for frequently called numbers and someone to dial for me and get people on the phone when I'm busy.

— I am way low on the totem pole when it comes to getting any cooperation from the secretarial and clerical staff. Typing letters, delivering faxes, getting documents from my client files, filing, etc. is pulling teeth. Frankly, I need a secretary to give me priority, even if I share her/him with someone else.

— My billing system and income records are not compatible with your financial system. Your accounting department is grudgingly sympathetic, but they are not doing anything about it.

— We have to have a procedure for the continuing development of my client base so as to generate increased income. This isn't on stream yet, and it doesn't look like it will be as it stands now.

This has to be put into play right away. I must see it starting to happen by next week. Friday, at the latest.

We went over what has to be done during our merger discussions, but hardly anything has been accomplished. You, not me, must talk to your people about this and see that it gets done. It probably means adding two or three persons to attend to my needs. A small expense when you consider the stakes.

Frankly, I did not come here to work harder, longer, and angrier. The promised state of affairs was to be the reverse of this.

It all adds up to one thing. I am unhappy. I don't intend to continue to be unhappy.

Make me happy!

Sheila Epps

Counter a Damaging Rumor That Could Halt Your Career.

Situation: You were recently appointed a partner at a high-powered law firm and are steadily and hopefully moving up to the management circle. You supervise an important account, a well-known auto rental company. Fees are up, and the client is happy.

You get word through the grapevine that a couple of the staff people and perhaps your assistant have whispered in the ear of the top managing partner that you at times denigrate him to your client—that you talk about getting unintelligent advice that hampers you. One snitch said you used the word "stupid."

You have, at times, been carried away in conversations with your client. Remarks such as this were taken out of context and tattled, undoubtedly for self-serving reasons. You are by no means disloyal or disrespectful of the firm's management.

You know that these leaks will mark you for extinction when the timing is right. At the very least, any chance of moving up is now down the drain. You must counteract this bad-mouthing straight out, with absolute certainty. At the same time, use the occasion to climb another rung or two up the ladder.

Strategy: Tell your client's top people that it would be good to meet with the firm's managing partner. Set up a lunch date at a classy restaurant, or, if they prefer, their conference room. (They opt for the lunch.) Send a memo to your president saying that your client's brass asked if he would meet with them.

The reason: You had been speaking so highly of your top boss, saying that he comes up with much of the ingenious legal thinking that you present, that they want to show their admiration firsthand and also to ask his advice on certain important issues. This is to be a command performance by your commander in chief. Don't indicate any knowledge of the venomous whisperings in his ear.

This will clearly make the bad-mouthing seem ludicrous, an unfounded attack against you for vicious reasons.

September 13, 1993

To: Edgar Ebersol, President

From: Barry Levin

Mr. Ebersol, may I prevail upon you for a favor?

Ravenal's management would very much like to meet with you. May I set this up? It would be nice to do it as a luncheon meeting, if it is okay with you.

You see, I get together with them once or twice a week to make sure the acquisition programs we drafted for them are moving ahead. Naturally, I give a lot of the credit to you. You are known as the seminal figure behind the scenes.

Now they are anxious to sit down and chat with you about their up-and-coming goals and some business problems that need high-level thinking.

I hope this doesn't put too much of a dent in your time schedule. These are nice guys, heading up a very nice client. And naturally, I want to put the firm's best foot forward whenever the chance comes up.

Can you give me two or three dates convenient to you? I'll coordinate it with their availability. I'll fill you in beforehand on the background and what will probably come up at the meeting.

Thanks so much.

Barry Levin

Try to Protect Your Company from Adverse Financial Scrutiny.

Situation: You are a senior officer and board member at a real estate investment company, which, for the past two years, has been going through tough times and financial losses. It was decided to restructure the various operations with consequent accounting adjustments that will "improve" the balance sheet. This is technically legal, but would it be considered a fair assessment of financial worth? Would it be credible to the media and the public?

Strategy: The year-end audit and financial report are coming up soon, and you have been in long sessions with the partner at the CPA firm who is doing the job. You explained the need for your corporate restructuring—which he, among others, took part in—and its impact on your financial statement.

   This is a crucial report, sure to have unusual scrutiny in the industry and the media. You would prefer to have the partner who did your previous audits handle this rather than another partner or another firm.

   Your company must come out as being forthright and clean. The accounting partner on your audit said he would cooperate with your financial people while adhering to sound professional standards.

   The audit was completed with desired results. The income figures do not cause raised eyebrows. There is no gossip of cooking the books, even though a number of adjustments were made.

   You will send a letter thanking the partner who is responsible for the audit. It puts on record that he did it with objective precision and adherence to the highest professional standards. In other words, the letter confirms that the audit was done in a fair and proper manner, just in case a competitor, the media, or a government bureau asks any questions.

September 10, 1993

Jordan K. Tramiel
Partner
Jensen, Logan Certified Public Accountants

_____

_____

Dear Jordan:

You did an excellent job on our 1993 audit, which will be included in our 1994 annual report. It warrants a special round of applause because of the great care you took on the financial adjustments that had to be made as a result of our corporate restructuring, a new acquisition, and a sale of assets.

You handled it with complete objectivity, and the income figures are reliable in accordance with the highest professional standards, as you pointed out. Furthermore, it was completed on time. This report will be the guidepost for our upcoming audits.

Please thank your staff for us.

Best wishes,

BARNET HARRIS

Barnet Harris
Sr. Vice President
Lawrence Securities

cc: Hortense Altshell (Jensen, Logan)
JoAnn Guilfoyle (Jensen, Logan)
Lamont Jones (Lawrence Securities)
Sylvia Roth (Lawrence Securities)

Upsetting a Highly Popular Undertaking with a Jarring Note of Caution.

Situation: You are the VP of sales at one of the reigning home appliance manufacturers. The company is also a player in the automotive field with its air conditioners and heaters.

The company has been in serious negotiations to buy out a large manufacturer of auto and truck tires, Amalgamated Rubber Co. This has been taking place on and off for three months, and it now appears that a deal is coming up. It's been widely covered in the press.

The tire company has a long-standing popular brand, the Road King line, which is number one in many markets and number two in others, but never less than third.

Amalgamated's conquering hero right now is their X-99 line, recently introduced with a big, costly advertising splash along with wide press coverage. It's a premium-priced high-performance product with a unique safety feature, a patented wet-dry tread.

Your top management and their outside financial and legal experts have been poking through Amalgamated's books, which look okay. Their sales and profits go up and down in this cyclical market, but long range, the revenues are healthy.

Amalgamated is a well-known brand with a good consumer franchise. X-99 looks like a sure success and is expected to give profits a nice push skyward. This is starting to be reflected in the most recent financial data because of heavy introductory shipments.

What has especially excited everyone is the symbiosis of the two companies. Amalgamated has clout with aftermarket retailers, including the big chains, which will help the sales of your company's auto appliances.

Strategy: You decided, with the okay of the marketing VP, to get a quick update on Amalgamated's market status. This is to be an informal check that gets behind the financials and the formal market reports that are put out by Amalgamated in their ebullient style. There were no suspicions of any cover-up in their reports; an exploratory check just seemed to be a judicious move.

You personally visited four of the biggest retail auto supply chains that stock Amalgamated. Combined, they do an enormous tire business. Your stature with a major company gave you an entree. Obviously, you didn't reveal the purpose. You were just checking out the tire market, curious about how the various brands were doing, including Amalgamated.

What you found out was startling. You were stunned by the X-99 quality problem in their last two shipments. Also, Amalgamated's bellwether Road King line was starting to slip in market share. This information was given by almost all the key people at the four companies you visited. They represent an imposing segment of total U.S. tire sales.

You told the marketing VP about this, and it was decided that you should immediately send a confidential letter to the chairman/CEO, with a copy to go to the president and, of course, the marketing VP who is your comrade-in-arms.

The bearer of ill tidings must thoroughly document his case. You prepared a report with the names and verbatim statements of everyone you spoke with. If any are called, you are sure they will confirm the gist of what they had told you. Your findings are incontrovertible.

IN-HOUSE MEMO TO YOUR CHAIRMAN

April 21, 1994   CONFIDENTIAL

Mr. Richard Hamilton, Chairman & CEO
Harrison Manufacturing, Inc.

_____

_____

From: Arthur Leland, VP Sales

Subject: Important Information in Regard to the Proposed Amalgamated Tire Acquisition.

cc: Leland Nesser, President
             Charles De Wonin, VP & CFO
             Kathleen Bauman, VP Marketing

I have discussed with Ms. Bauman certain information I found out about Amalgamated, and we decided that I should bring it to your attention as quickly as possible.

I dislike being a fly in the ointment, as I know we are in an advanced stage on the Amalgamated buyout, but this could have a material effect on your thinking.

Kathleen Bauman and I felt that I should visit several of Amalgamated's large direct accounts and talk with key people there about what they thought of the company, its products, and any other concerns. I spoke with their merchandise managers, buyers, and retail sales managers. This was to be an informal check to give us an updated reflection of the company's current status.

These are the companies I called on:

> Beelo Stores, Los Angeles
> Barrow Auto Supplies, St. Louis
> Keystone Service, Chicago
> Hildenbrand's, New York

The information from these auto aftermarket giants certainly gives us a good view of Amalgamated's situation right at the firing line—and precisely now, when it counts.

- The two most recent shipments of their new X-99 line had 5 percent to 7 percent defects, which is unacceptable. It consisted of a weakness near the rim that resulted in small fissures. Some were detected before application to wheels, others happened between 50 and 150 miles of use. It's quite possible there will be other such occurrences after 500, 1,000, or 5,000 miles.

As you see, there's a chance there may have to be a recall of some sorts. I don't know how many tires are involved, but it could be substantial enough to be alarming. I do not know what Amalgamated is doing about this. Suffice it to say, the dealers consider it to be serious.

- It has caused these dealers to lose confidence in Amalgamated. They are holding customers off on buying X-99 until this quality problem is fixed.
- Two competitive brands are cutting into Amalgamated's biggest-selling line, Road King, because of their somewhat lower retail prices and equal quality. This is because retailers can make better customer deals on these brands because of higher markups and promotional allowances. It's a cutthroat business in which, I believe, Amalgamated is losing market share.
- All these retailers came through with similar comments.

Coming out with caveats at this late stage does not make one popular. But Kathleen and I know this intelligence alert is important for you to have in your pocket as you continue discussions with Amalgamated.

It took me three weeks to get all this and confirm it, which is why I'm bringing it to you now. Obviously, better now than never.

Very truly yours,

Arthur Leland

Arthur Leland

P.S. I transcribed the verbatim comments of all the people I spoke with. These are in a thirty-one-page report that I'm sending you under separate cover.

Senior Executives Decide to Rise Up and Present a Complaint about the President to the Company Chairman.

Situation: You are a senior executive at a machine tool manufacturer. The president of the company has become insufferable. His treatment of key executives has deteriorated through the years to where he is now an abusive martinet. He takes sport in beating down and insulting people in front of their peers.

Weekend meetings are called on short notice, most often unnecessarily. He makes dawn and late-night calls to employees' homes. The executives are shaky and afraid to make decisions. It's impossible to do a creditable job.

The key executives suffering this torture select you as their spokesman to talk to the board chairman. You phoned him, and he listened attentively. He then asked you to specify your complaints in a letter to him.

On the record, the president has been very good for the company. During his five-year term profits increased by over 50 percent and net worth doubled. This makes serious denunciations particularly touchy. They could easily be sloughed off as bellyaching.

The chairman assured you that whatever you say will not prejudice you or the executives making this charge, provided it is factual, objective, and free of passion or invective.

Strategy: This situation calls for a businesslike letter stating the germane points without specific details. Leave this for a follow-up if and when the chairman asks for it.

You are putting yourself on the line. Reiterate the chairman's pledge that this will not affect your standing in the company or that of the others in the rebel group.

LETTER TO THE CHAIRMAN

November 22, 1993   PRIVATE AND CONFIDENTIAL

Mr. Aubrey C. Hormeyer
Chairman of the Board
Clifton Industries, Inc.

_____

_____

Dear Mr. Hormeyer:

At your request, I am stating, on behalf of myself and the other senior executives listed below, certain serious complaints about Mr. Randall Gordon.

It concerns the insulting and abusive manner with which he confronts us and his inability to clearly guide the direction of this company. This seriously affects our performance, and we believe is detrimental to the corporate welfare.

I was selected by the executive staff to be their spokesman in bringing this to your attention. It is an extremely disturbing task for me personally and, certainly, for all of us. It is acknowledged that during the five years of Mr. Gordon's tenure Clifton's net profits rose by 56 percent, and the stock price doubled.

Mr. Gordon holds a full-scale meeting twice a week to review our activities. We have come to call these meetings inquisitions. They start out as business discussions. But for no reason, Mr. Gordon will often fly into a rage, with loud outbursts, criticisms, and personal insults. Most often no significant directives are being made. The result is that there is no unified corporate policy.

His numerous calls for unnecessary weekend meetings and phone calls to our homes at all hours are legendary, even outside the company.

This type of treatment is stifling and prevents us from being able to perform at our best. It is disruptive to the people who report to us.

At this time, I will not go into detail as to specific incidents. We can furnish this if requested.

We feel it is our duty to bring this information to you. It is in the spirit of acting to the benefit of Clifton Industries, the board of directors, and our shareholders.

You assured me that this will not be prejudicial to me or to the others shown here, who have seen this letter and share its conviction.

Thank you for viewing this with interest.

Very truly yours,

Harvey T. Sigler

c.c.   Guy Baxter, VP
       Hilda Forrest, VP   Harvey T. Sigler
       George Maxwell, VP   Vice President, Merchandising
       Audrey Peters, VP

Protect Your Flanks *from Outside Dangers*—Clients, Vendors, etc.

A Change of Command at Your Best Customer. You Must Get in Solid.

Situation: You are a principal at a TV production company. A large cable TV operator is your best customer by far. They have put in someone new to replace your former contact, a close friend who was fired. You now have a new de facto chief, who okays your bills and can keep you on or dismiss you. Your mission: Get close to this guy.

He is a headstrong catalyst, scurrying about and making sweeping changes. You don't want to be swept out. You've got to meet with him quickly, but he's hard to pin down and difficult to speak with on the phone. What's more, he doesn't know you. Worse: You know he has a favorite production house that he worked with before and who can ease you out of the picture.

Strategy: Send your new client lead-man a letter asking for a meeting. Imply that you had been previously throttled in bringing them creative programming concepts but that now you'll be able to show them great, trend-setting entertainment ideas.

In order to assure a positive meeting ambience, which will get you off on the right foot, you have to cater to his ego, which you were told is immense. You arrange for an executive of the Cable TV Trade Association to be with you at the meeting. You say in the letter that this trade official wants to be there to get the benefit of your client's thoughts on the future of cable and how the industry can progress more rapidly. Your client's comments will be in the association journal and distributed to the news media, which you have arranged through a PR agency.

This is the red herring that will make your client want to see you. You are able to hoist his stature. He is on an ego trip. You have served him well.

LETTER TO THE CLIENT

December 16, 1993

Mr. C. Carter Barrow
Executive Vice President
Cable Television Systems, Inc.

_____

_____

Dear Mr. Barrow:

Congratulations on taking the helm! It will be wonderful working for you. You'll now see imaginative programming concepts we previously weren't in a position to present to CTS because of so many inhibiting restrictions.

Depending on your schedule, we want to meet with you as soon as possible to get your thinking on the future direction of CTS. In this way, we'll be better able to target our output. We can be an arm of CTS, an effective tool for carrying out your strategy.

Understandably, you've been extremely busy, so it's been hard to pin you down. The executive VP and another official of the U.S. Cable Association want to join us when we get together. They are anxious to get the benefit of your thinking on the status of the industry and the direction they should take as a trade association.

I believe they want to feature your comments in a news release to the media. Since you are a celebrated spokesperson for the industry, your opinions will have weight.

We, and the U.S. Cable Association, are looking forward to our meeting. I'll call to arrange the date.

Best wishes,

A Faithful Client Is Now Speaking with Another Vendor and Having Them Compete with You for a Job Assignment. It Has Never Happened Before.

Situation: You, a VP at a data-processing firm, have a long and extraordinarily amicable relationship with an important client, a supermarket chain. They are in the habit of handing you assignments, big or small, whenever the need comes up. You are steady, reliable, trustworthy, and always come through. Now, suddenly, another company got into the act to present ideas for an assignment. Why?

Your client contact may be doing it to demonstrate to his management that he looks at more than one proposal, more than one bid. That he checks out new suppliers. Did he get pressure from higher up? You are anxious and fearful.

Strategy: Send a letter stating that each one of the client's requests is taken as a new challenge, with completely new thinking. In keeping with this, you are assigning new people in your company to this next assignment. It's your normal procedure.

Some will be free-lancers to get entirely new faces and minds into the act. You need these extra bodies to supplement your small staff. The experience and knowledge of your regular account staff is a valuable backup.

In this way, your client will have fresh outside thinking, which is augmented by people with a thorough knowledge of their business—more than a match for your competitor.

You must give this client assurance and confidence—in you personally and in the ideas you show them. You don't want them to become enamored of new flash-in-the-pan spectacular schemes a competitor may put in front of them.

LETTER TO THE CLIENT

April 15, 1994

Ms. Geraldine DeLucas
Vice President
Deserving Supermarkets, Inc.

_____

_____

Re: Limited Network Proposal

Dear Gerrie:

Thanks so much for this latest assignment. You know we've always come through for you before, and I'm sure you are confident we'll do it again.

This letter is not to blow our horn. It's a routine message we send to our valued clients every so often just to let them know how we operate. And why you can depend on us to come up with fresh ideas and get your jobs done right. Our ideas are not just flashes. Each one comes about in accordance with a special process we have here to make sure it is not just an innovation, but a practical innovation, an innovation that works.

As an example, this new assignment will be put to a group here who haven't worked on your business before. They are unencumbered by past proposals and past thinking. Their mission is to brainstorm fresh ways of doing this job. They bring the perspectives of other industries with similar types of problems. We rotate the personnel on your projects in this way.

The people who regularly handle your account—the regulars we call them—will stay in the background and not interfere. We don't want to introduce any preconceived notions at the beginning that may inhibit new thinking.

The regulars are very important because of their experience with your company. They know your policies, industry policies, regulations, the history of what worked well before, what didn't work, and why. And of course they are very capable of fresh thinking.

We'll show you all the refreshingly new ideas. Some, we may say, are not practical, but we want you to look them over anyway. An approach may sound glamorous and fascinatingly innovative, but for a good reason it may be a wild-eyed scheme that won't work. Worse, it might cost you time, money, and reputation if you went ahead with it. What we bring to the table is creativity, knowledge, and experience.

Thanks for taking the time to read this, Gerrie. I thought you'd be interested in knowing of our policy in handling all your assignments, including, of course, this latest one.

Best regards,

Find Out the Pecking Order and Sensors Before Commencing Work for a New Client.

Situation: You, a partner in a big-time accounting firm, just got a new client. To help assure a smooth start and ease the transition from their previous firm, you should know who at the company does what and when, who is in charge of what, who does what to whom, etc. It's an involuted circle with spirals and whorls, wound around an axis.

Knowing it will avoid backbiting, turf wars, stepping on toes, and costly frustrations, not to mention excessive overtime. Your client will be happier. You will be successful with the account.

Strategy: Write the CFO, your top contact, whom you have known for several years, and tell him your shop has started the wheels turning on his account. But in order to avoid problems and maximize efficiency, you should know what is not shown on the personnel flowchart, the behind-the-scenes picture.

Do this at dinner, in a pleasant, relaxed ambience, accompanied by good food and wine, where candor and goodwill has a way of unfolding. *In vino veritas.*

LETTER TO THE CLIENT

September 16, 1993

Mr. Timothy Rogers Saunders
Senior Vice President, Chief Financial Officer
Locus Electronic, Inc.

_____

_____

Dear Tim:

It is the ultimate in understatement to tell you we are delighted to have won your business. It was a long, hard road. And I thank you for the part you played.

Now we go to work, and we're looking forward to showing you and your colleagues what we can do.

As a prelude, I think it would be productive to sit down together and put into focus the people and places, aside from you, who will be involved—even peripherally—in what we do. Obviously, you are our boss, but because your time is valuable, we don't want to bother you with questions if others could give the answers.

In a nutshell, it would be helpful to know the pecking order: Who has the antennas, where they point, and how far up or sideways they go.

Flowcharts are fine, but it's also good to get filled in on what's behind the charts. It's kind of a third-dimensional look at the folks in the squares as well as behind and around them—where the egos and alter egos lie.

Tim, let's have dinner next week to go over all of this. Any evening that's right for you is fine with me. If not next week, please give me your next open date.

Thanks so much for your confidence. It's going to be great working for you.

Warm regards,

Keep Your Customers' Loyalty After Your Company Was Taken Over.

Situation: You own a reputable insurance brokerage in a wealthy suburb, with a sizable customer base, acquired throughout sixty years of much sweat and little leisure, in good times and bad. You now have a comfortably profitable operation.

It's time to make things easier. You negotiated with a much larger insurance brokerage to be swept into their operation. Your income directly depends on the retention of your customers and their continuing loyalty.

Strategy: Announce the merger to your customers as a good move for them and for you. It will assure the continuation of the excellent service you've provided and even enhance it through a wider range of insurance carriers and more backup support and expertise. Plus, you'll have a lot more strength in the industry. The bottom line is they'll get the best protection for their needs at the most favorable prices.

Further, as tangible proof that they will get the same personal service from you as before—that they are not being given over to strangers—your key people are moving with you to handle their business. Your customers can call you at the same phone number. Everything is the same, only bigger and better.

LETTER TO YOUR CUSTOMERS

February 8, 1994

Mr. Zish Monteveld
Monteveld Restaurant Supplies

—————————————

—————————————

Dear Mr. Monteveld:

WE'RE MOVING . . . WE'RE BIGGER

On May 1, our offices will be relocated to 103 Charter Boulevard, Secaucus, New Jersey. At that time, Schein/Michaels will become a major division of Marshall Insurance Counselors, one of the biggest independent insurance brokerage firms on the East Coast.

We'll have the same name, the same phone and fax numbers, and the same people in charge of your account. The same voices will answer the phone when you call. You will have the same personal service and attention you need and deserve. . . .

And, in addition, you will have access to many extra benefits. For example:

— A much broader range of insurance carriers will enable us to secure the best coverage for all of your insurance needs . . . at the best prices.

— Full service Life, Health, Group, Estate Planning, and Employee Benefits departments will be able to handle all of these requirements, *in house*—a cost savings.

— You'll get additional backup and support from a combined firm with a large professional staff having expertise in all fields of insurance, a firm that has a great deal of clout in the insurance industry today.

The bottom line is that as insurance coverage becomes more varied and complex (and, yes, more confusing to the customer) you will be assured of the best protection for your needs and the best service . . . at the lowest prices. And again, your account will continue to be handled by the same people, the people you know and can rely on.

We'll be in touch with you shortly. Meanwhile, as always, we're looking forward to your call any time you have a question or need service.

Warm regards,

Larry Schein

Larry Schein
President
Schein/Michaels & Marshall

The Second-Tier Managers at Your Client Are Undermining You. Fight It.

Situation: You are a senior management supervisor at an ad agency. Your major responsibility is a big-name packaged foods company, located two and a half jet hours away. Your influence with your client is beamed right to the top—the corporate chairman, president, and EVP. That's your strength. Your day-to-day dealings, however, are with middle management.

Your power with the ivory tower rankles the midmanagement. They bitterly resent the greater access you have to their commanders than they enjoy. Their power over you is theoretical. Their authority as ''the client to be feared'' is subverted. Indeed, you are a threat.

The midmanagement mission is to make you look bad, to get you off center stage. They do everything possible to put traps in your path. This is done by intention, by impulse, and by instinct, but always with a seemingly earnest desire to help you.

You are in a spot because you have to deal with these people every day. Their job is to give you orders, to certify what you do, and approve your bills for doing it.

You have a distinct disadvantage: They are in day-to-day contact with the powers, in a position to frequently report about your performance. You don't know what they say, and you are not around to defend yourself.

Strategy: The time has come to make a move. You have strength with the power center. Use it before you are discredited. Take action before the situation is untenable. As Hugh Walpole stated in one of his writings: ''Don't play for safety. It's the most dangerous game in the world.''

Call one of your top-brass admirers, the EVP in charge of the entire department you work with. Briefly mention your problem without making a big deal of it on the phone.

Next, send a letter, indicating you are bringing up the same problem you had previously spoken about on the phone and that can eventually hurt her. Give some detail. You want to be helpful. Make a date to see her on other matters and on this one too, when you will spell out all the facts.

This is not a brouhaha. This is guerrilla warfare. Map your tactics, then launch your assault.

LETTER TO YOUR CLIENT

April 21, 1994

Ms. Annamarie Lucia Alvarez
Executive Vice President, Consumer Marketing
Succulent Foods Corp.

_____

_____

Dear Annamarie:

Annamarie, there is a problem in your marketing department that is causing some turmoil and is costing you money. I touched on it briefly on the phone last week without going into detail.

We've been meeting our assignment deadlines promptly and submitting great work. It seems that most of the deadlines we get are unrealistically and unnecessarily tight. We get last-minute work orders to be completed in a week or two, or even in a few days, that should ordinarily take three or four weeks. We're told there is a dire urgency, so we pull out all stops. Like a fire department, we've been on call from emergency to emergency.

That's not all. Sometimes when we deliver the work, it just sits there. Nothing is done about it for two or three weeks. Sometimes never. As in the fire department, there are false alarms.

I don't have to tell you what this costs in overtime and wear and tear on our people and yours. We're coping, admirably well, but I'm afraid that this lack of good organization is going to hurt your business.

Annamarie, we're here to carry out your needs. We submitted plans and we submitted schedules, which everyone agreed on. Naturally, there are last-minute urgencies, fires to put out. It's the nature of the business, and what we are good at. But it seems that there could have been more upfront notice on at least some of the "emergencies."

I don't get to see you much, since we're a thousand miles apart. I'd like to hop over next week to go over a number of things. And at the same time, we can discuss what I brought up here. I'll call to set the date.

Warm regards,

Getting Back into the Good Graces of a Client After Being Declared *Persona Non Grata.*

Situation: You are a staff writer for a big public relations agency. A major client is an international construction company for whom you produce releases and articles.

There was a meeting at the client's offices to present an article you had written for one of their divisions. You were carried away and became a bit too forceful in presenting your work, with a hint of irritation in your tone and body language when they voiced some differences with what you presented. It annoyed the client's division manager to the point where she told the agency's VP and account director not to have you there again.

It's ironic, because your work was well received, even praised. It was an issue of attitude, not talent. Naturally, it's a shock, a severe blow to your professional pride. Needless to say, your standing in the agency is greatly diminished.

Strategy: The first step was to phone the client manager who declared you an out-person to find out why—you know it's not the quality of your work. Your goal was to set it right. After clearing it within the agency, you made the call. It turned out well. She mentioned the reason for her displeasure—you were out of order by displaying a vexatious attitude. She agreed to rescind her dictum. What a relief!

It's important for you to follow up with a letter to her. You don't want to grovel or be overly subservient. You must maintain a professional persona and be apologetic yet dignified.

The letter is the charming tidbit that will elevate your standing with this important client manager. You will have bonded.

LETTER TO THE CLIENT

January 25, 1994

Ms. Felicia Parker
Division Manager
Hatfield, Morgan Construction, International, Inc.

———————————

———————————

Dear Felicia:

I was so glad we chatted yesterday. And thanks so much for helping me understand why I irked you to the point of declaring me *persona non grata*.

It was not my work, which you really liked. I feel good about this.

It was my attitude of being too assertive and impatient. I feel very bad about this.

It was an outpouring of zeal, and this time it was displayed too energetically. A bad error. Thank you for forgiving it.

As said by two very wise people:

"Zeal is very blind, or badly regulated, when it encroaches upon the rights of others" (Quesnel)
"To err is human, to forgive divine" (Alexander Pope)

It's good to be working with you.

Best regards,

Hattie Weinberg

Hattie Weinberg

Your Presentation for Some Juicy New Business Seems Dead. Lower Your Cost to Revive It—and Look Credible.

Situation: You're the head of an insurance brokerage office that made an all-out pitch for a big new account. It would raise your premium income by 25 percent, with little extra overhead. Your present staff plus two additional people could handle it.

    The scuttlebutt says that you are not getting it. Two other brokers appear to be neck-and-neck in the lead, with you a bit behind. This translates to O-U-T.

Strategy: You will not give up. You have nothing to lose by pulling out all the stops and giving it the extra effort. You have to find some way to kindle their interest and give it a new life.

    What better way could there be than by reducing their premium by a sizable amount? It will undercut your competition. You sharpen your pencil and plead with your insurance suppliers. You cut your profits. You desperately want to make this deal. It will give you entree to more of this company's insurance business, which can be lucrative. But you must explain, in a credible way, why you didn't quote this lower premium originally.

    Start with an E-mail dispatch to get immediate attention and to halt a commitment with another broker if it is imminent. Follow up with a fax the same day. Then send the fax original as a letter, with a prominent line on top, *Original of Previous Fax.*

    You will get the message out quickly and dramatically, and you'll have a document for the record. You've done everything practicable to latch on to this business. You smoothed the way for the gods to smile on you. Now hope they do.

E-MAIL TO THE PROSPECTIVE CLIENT

October 4, 1993

To: Mrs. Helena Packard Estes
        Coalition Real Estate Management, Inc.

From: Manning Tilden, President
        Babcok & Tilden Insurance

A new insurance package came up yesterday. It will save you a great deal of money on your premium—with the same coverage. We have an exclusive on this now. A fax will follow today with details.

Manning Tilden

October 4, 1993   *By Fax: Original to Follow*

Mrs. Helena Packard Estes
Executive Vice President
Coalition Real Estate Management, Inc.

_____

_____

Dear Mrs. Estes:

Things changed for the better since we gave you our proposal two weeks ago.
Better for you. Much better.

There have been changes in certain insurance rates in the last two weeks that
make it possible for us to bring the premium estimate we quoted before down by
$42,300 a year—for the same coverage. This means you can have a clear savings
of $42,300 a year from what you were previously quoted before.

We're never static. We're constantly on the lookout for new insurance packages,
new regulations, new coverages, new pricing. This is to make sure our clients
always have the right protection at the best prices. They get the benefit of the
latest advantages the moment they become available.

We decided to put two executives and a claims technician on your account as their
priority responsibility. You will always have an expert on call. In addition, I or my
associate will be visiting your office from time to time. As the head of this firm, I
assume the responsibility of making sure you get the best possible service. I am
available to you anytime.

It would be good for us to come in to discuss this new coverage and the special low
rate plan. How about this coming Thursday, October 7? I'll call you to confirm.

Very truly yours,

The Odds Are Stacked Against You on a Client Acquisition Presentation. Try Hard to Improve Your Chances.

Situation: You are the sales manager at a communications systems company, hungrily eager to get your foot in the door at a dominant cable network. An opportunity comes up. They are looking for a new communications procedure—just your specialty. Nailing down this project, or at least a part of it, would be a marvelous triumph.

You camped at the doorstep of the decision maker and pleaded/talked your way into a presentation meeting. You got the date, as a courtesy really, as a result of your persistence and personality.

You worked hard at producing a sterling presentation, with money-saving ideas and foolproof backup systems. This was your chance and you had to make the most of it.

Your competition are two vendors he has been working with for years. They are heavy with talent and dependable—the old reliables. Your prospect trusts them. He is comfortable with them. Edging your way in is tough.

Your meeting didn't click—you felt it, knew it. Your sales target was polite, even jovial, but he kept looking at his watch. His eyes were glazed, and he stared out the window a couple of times. You were a newcomer, a stranger not being taken seriously.

You gave him the highlights of your outstanding presentation. You caught his interest. But you couldn't get enough time to deliver your entire story. Your full pitch was in a binder that you handed him.

He probably will not review it seriously. All your preparation, your exquisite ideas, and your powerful prose are down the drain. You think. No, you are certain.

Strategy: It's crazy to give up, considering all the brains and sweat you put into it. This has to go another round.

Send a letter cajoling him into giving you another meeting date. Tell him you admire his sagacity in wanting to go beyond the vendors he's used for so long. He will get a gold mine of fresh ideas, a new look, by adding your creative company to his privileged supplier clique. You want to massage his ego without seeming to be gratuitously flattering.

The odds of a second meeting are stacked against you, but you've got to give it a big try.

LETTER TO THE CLIENT PROSPECT

October 26, 1993

Mr. Jeffrey A. O'Neil
Senior Vice President
FSA Cable Systems

_____

_____

Re: Communications System Revamping

Dear Mr. O'Neil:

> "Genius . . . means little more than the faculty of
> perceiving in an unhabitual way." (William James)

Having us make our presentation was admirable. Shall I say a flash of genius?

We're not in your present vendor circle, not one of the people you are used to having handle your communication needs. Familiarity brings comfort. It also brings sameness, stodginess, and old ideas being regenerated, refurbished, and revamped, but seldom totally replaced. Not invented from scratch.

You want a new look, another perspective, a new way of solving a problem. I'm sure that's why you agreed to see what we can do. It took boldness, but that's the way you break out of the mold and get innovative ideas.

Our proposal was put together in our usual careful, deliberate way. It was thoughtfully conceived and displays a creative concept for carrying out your assignment with the use of cutting-edge technology. Something like this was never done before. Think of the extra value this adds to your network.

Our reputation tells you that you can count on us to do the job above expectations. We always do what we say we will—and then some—on time and within the budget.

May we see you again briefly to give you more insight into our previous proposal? As well as several new thoughts that came to us as a result of our meeting? Just a few minutes is all we ask. If we are privileged to win this business, or any part of it, you will have a refreshingly new vendor.

Best regards,

You Can't Agree to Your Client's Unreasonable Request. Appease Them.

Situation: You are the president of a marketing research company and have just completed a consumer survey, ordered and paid for by an advertising agency. The purpose was to find out the effectiveness of their current campaign for an important client, a fast-foods chain.

The figures show the ads to be *somewhat* effective. Clearly, there is room for improvement, and the research data suggests ways to do it.

The agency's supervisor on the account is unhappy about the data in your elegantly bound report and suggested certain small changes that would mitigate some of the more unpleasant findings. He noted it would help temper "confusion and bias" in the study.

Strategy: You obviously cannot accede to this request. The product of your business is truth and objectivity. Let the chips fall where they may. The integrity of your work cannot be compromised. It could mean death to your reputation and your business. Nevertheless, this is a good client, and you are obliged to show a spirit of cooperation.

Send your client a letter pointing out that all you provided are cold figures, which are subject to analysis and interpretation. The agency could interpret them in their own way to show they are doing an adequate job. You don't have to be brought into this. It's between them and their client.

Most importantly, the agency should demonstrate how the research points the way to further improving the advertising. After all, this was the purpose of the research. The agency couldn't take corrective steps until these findings were available.

Note that you'll be pleased to help the agency in the ad-improvement rationale. Suggest that they should display their ad face-lift to their client at the same time the research is presented. You will be most pleased to be at this meeting as a backup, if invited.

LETTER TO YOUR CLIENT

January 28, 1994

Mr. Brett Simon
Senior Vice President
Callan, Isprey Advertising Agency Inc.

_____

_____

Dear Brett:

The conversation we had yesterday reminds me of a saying in one of Aesop's fables: "Every truth has two sides. It is well to look at both, before we commit ourselves to either."

You acquired remarkable information from the consumer survey we delivered last Friday. It shows the agency has been doing a good job, but it also suggests areas of improvement. Let's face it, that's why you did the study. The purpose of the research was to determine how to make the commercial message more effective.

We did very little interpretation in our report. We simply showed the facts as they came out of our tabulations. The hard data can't change, of course. We have no control over that. I know you agree that it's our business to present the findings as they are.

Here's another wise saying, this one by Henry Clay: "Statistics are no substitute for judgment."

As I indicated before, the figures should be interpreted in a way that points to how the ads could be strengthened. I suggest that you make a full-blown presentation of your recommendations to your client at the same time that you display the research. They are unquestionably much more interested in your creative work than in the cold research facts.

You can count on our full cooperation in backing you up. I'll be glad to consult on your presentation, and I'll attend your client meeting with you if you wish.

Regards,

You Can't Make the Deadline on an Important Assignment for a New Client.

Situation: You are a partner in a sales promotion and package design firm and have been aching for years to get in the door of a famous cosmetics company. Finally, there's a call from them. They need a design overhaul of one of their popular lines plus a trade brochure announcing the change.

There is a three-month deadline. It's extremely tight, but you don't want to blow this chance of finally getting cozy with this company. You feel you can do it with an all-out crash effort.

The time constraint they imposed is necessary to get the designs plus the brochure copy and layout into the hands of the people who will produce it so as to make a retail store delivery date nine months hence. Everything has to be coordinated with pinpoint timing. You are doing the initial stage, and all else that follows depends on your work coming through on time.

You are two and a half months into the job and you see you can't make the three-month deadline. You need two additional weeks. It's not because you fell down on the job; you made the best possible effort. There were just not enough hours in the day.

Strategy: Send a letter. Say that you are doing this work on a crash basis but without compromising quality. You have to lodge the thought that the schedule will be met even though the final part of the job will be delivered two weeks after the deadline date. The letter must be positive.

Say that you will deliver all the graphics and packaging copy on time for review by the marketing, legal, and lab people. This will include final designs on 90 percent of the packages. It will take the client's people about two weeks to review all this. And they can then pass it on for the start of production. They will receive the rest two weeks later, so that production will keep moving along without a hitch. The production schedule will not be held up.

For all practical purposes the deadline has been met. No time will be lost. You came through on this very difficult assignment.

LETTER TO THE CLIENT

January 28, 1994

Ms. Olivia de la Portega
President
Cashmere Cosmetics Associates, Inc.

_____

_____

Dear Olivia:

You gave us the impossible. We are coming through.

More important, there is no compromise, not the least bit, on quality. Not just quality alone, but perfection. Because that's how we do every assignment. Proof? Your people are seeing it as they follow the work taking place in our shop. You will soon see it too.

Here is the schedule:

> You want designs and copy ready by February 16 so that it can be passed on for your internal review—marketing, legal, and the lab. This will take two weeks. We'll have 90 percent of the package designs ready by this date. You can then start sending it to production on March 3.

> On March 2, we'll deliver the rest of the packaging and the brochure designs. This small part can then be reviewed internally and passed on without losing production time.

Your time schedule for getting this revamped line to market is intact insofar as our contribution is concerned. Despite the most difficult timing conditions imaginable and the most stringent quality standards, we made the deadline for getting all the packaging and brochure into production.

Job perfect. Mission accomplished.

Very truly yours,

Neutralize Unfavorable News to Your Client. Give It a Positive Slant.

Situation: You are a VP at an advertising agency, supervising a national fast-foods account. You commissioned a market research company to conduct a consumer survey in order to evaluate your new campaign. The data came in—not bad, but not good. How do you present it to your client?

Strategy: After all, the purpose of the research is to indicate how you can strengthen the campaign. You didn't have this consumer information before; you had to shoot from the hip. Considering this, your advertising can be considered pretty good under the circumstances. Now, at last, you have the material that will make it a smashing success.

You tell this to your client in a letter, knowing they are anxious to see the research findings. Mention that the data doesn't make sense until they see what you are doing about it. That's why, along with this research, you want to present the agency's recommendations for strengthening the advertising based on this new information.

LETTER TO YOUR CLIENT

June 14, 1994

Mr. Harry Sweeney
Vice President, Marketing
Fine & Healthy, Inc.

_____

_____

Dear Harry:

The research findings are coming in, and we're sifting through them. Right now, it's in the form of cold data and will not make any sense until it's analyzed, giving us direction on further strengthening the new campaign.

Don't forget, we didn't have the benefit of this information when we built the strategy because we had to get started quickly, in time for your new TV programming. What's running now is the first stage, and it looks like we're on the right track.

Now, by virtue of the research, we will give the advertising the finishing touches. This will be presented next week along with the research. How is Friday, June 23, 11:00 A.M. in our conference room? Please let me know who will attend. We'll have lunch prepared.

I'm sure you agree it makes sense to show everything at once. The research and the advertising creative work will have more meaning when you see them together.

Regards,

A Vendor Is Going over Your Head, Directly to Your Boss. Stop It Dead.

Situation: You head up an airline's maintenance purchasing department. An equipment company salesman has been showing his wares to you for the past fourteen months. Although he's been getting a cordial reception each time, you haven't put him into your inner circle of suppliers. His merchandise is good but not outstanding enough to take orders away from your coterie of suppliers.

   The salesman, looking to crack your account any way he can, served notice he will go directly to the senior VP of maintenance, to whom you report. You are concerned about the likelihood he will complain about the difficulty of breaking into your supplier network and point out to your boss that an outsider is unable to get a fair hearing.

Strategy: Here is a threat to your pleasant hegemony, to your strength in the company, your power over your suppliers. He must be blown away, nipped in the bud. His request must be dead on arrival.

   Send a memo to your boss warning him of the impending call from a disgruntled salesman who was turned down for good reason. Confirm your policy of purchasing the best products at the best prices and impartially investigating all reliable sources.

   This salesperson wants to undeservedly penetrate your wall of objective appraisal in an outlaw fashion. Advise your boss not to bother taking the call. It will needlessly take up his time, upset proper business routine, and could foment chaos in the purchasing operation.

MEMO TO YOUR BOSS

September 13, 1993

To: Mr. Herbert C. Michaels
        Senior Vice President, Maintenance
        Alliance Airlines, Inc.

From: Harry Krackower,
        Manager, Maintenance Purchasing Department

Dear Mr. Michaels:

This is to alert you to the probability that you may receive a phone call from an equipment distributor, GF Materials, in an attempt to display its product line to you personally.

This is unauthorized by me and indeed is in direct violation of what I told this supplier. In short, he is going over my head.

I don't have to tell you, Mr. Michaels, that this office carefully tests and screens each piece of equipment needed and negotiates the best possible price terms. Naturally, we can't buy from everyone. What we purchase, and from whom, is done strictly on merit—in terms of quality, on-time delivery, reliability, financial stability, reputation, etc.

The phone call to you will be from an unhappy salesperson who was turned down here because his products did not measure up to our standards for various reasons such as were cited before. His contemplated action is disruptive to our entire purchasing system as well as being a burden to your office.

In my opinion, it is best not to acknowledge this call. I'm sorry for the need to take up your time on this.

Regards,

Harry Krackower

You Want to Shake Up a Vendor. They Are Acting Too Cavalier.

Situation: The people at your PR agency show wry faces and look askance at some of your requests, the ones that are not routine and that require an extra effort. It's as if they're being punished. This is not a real problem because they do a good job. But it's unpleasant and has become irritating to you and your staff.

Strategy: Send a short letter to the head of the PR firm. Make it pleasant but pointed. Ruffle him. Let it be known that he'll have to change his employees' attitudes.

LETTER TO THE VENDOR

October 22, 1993

Ms. Mary Broder Stein
President
Semaphore Public Relations Associates

———————————————

———————————————

Dear Ms. Stein:

> "A smooth sea never made a skillful mariner."
> (English proverb)

It seems that some assignments we give your people are met with complaints. These are the ones that require a little more time and effort. We get such rejoinders as it's tough to do, it presents a problem, and so on.

It has gotten to the point where it's become tiresome and annoying. My folks are now complaining about it.

Mary, we assign you the things that you are in business for. We look to you to take care of our PR needs and problems, period. If they are easy, we don't need you. Our requests are not outlandish. After all, we don't ask you to run a restaurant or build a car factory.

This is not a big deal when you think about it. Your people are good, and we're pleased with your service. Why make it unpleasant at times? I simply think that now is the time to get this off my chest.

Be well,

A Local Zoning Variance Threatens Your Business. Get It Changed.

Situation: You own a popular restaurant on a busy shopping thoroughfare in a suburban town. The zoning commission is planning to authorize a walk-in shelter for the homeless—on your block. This is a do-good project for the community.

   You don't want it on your block or even in the immediate shopping area, where it will surely affect your patronage. Further, the extra turmoil and traffic will be a significant hazard to the many youngsters who frequent the area.

Strategy: Send a letter to the commission stating that although it's a commendable move, it would be totally unsuitable for your block.

   Also send a letter to other merchants in the area enlisting their support in making a formal protest to the commission and the town council.

LETTER TO THE ZONING COMMISSION

To: Zoning and Variance Commission
Town of North Haven

From: Barbara Schwartz, Owner of Barbara's Cafe, 104 Kennedy Road

Date: January 10, 1994

Re: Proposal for Converting 128 Kennedy Road to a Walk-in Shelter for the Homeless.

I applaud your cooperation with the county in making such a facility available for homeless people in our area.

Please consider, however, that it would be a serious error in having such an establishment at this address.

This part of Kennedy Road is a popular shopping promenade, frequented all day and evening by a great many adults and children, including many shoppers from outside this community.

This facility will significantly increase traffic on already busy streets—because of support facilities, staff activities, social services, and so on. It will endanger the many teenagers who gather and shop here. Further, the heavy traffic will put these homeless people at risk.

I urgently ask that you give your utmost consideration to placing such a center in a more appropriate location and avoid the inconvenience and danger it can cause at the location now being considered.

At the very least, I believe a research study should be conducted to determine the pedestrian flow and traffic congestion now and to ascertain the increase that will occur if such a facility is located here.

Very truly yours,

Barbara Schwartz

LETTER TO NEARBY MERCHANTS

January 10, 1994

Mr. Frank Martin
Kennedy Eye Glass Emporium

_____

_____

Dear Frank:

This is about the proposed center for the homeless to be established on our block. We talked about it and worried about it, but we never made a serious attempt to stop it because we figured it was some bad news that wouldn't happen.

Now it looks like it's happening. The proposal may very well go through.

I don't have to elaborate on the consequences to us. We all know of the big potential decline in shopper traffic and the reduced property values, of the traffic congestion and further parking problems in the already scarce spaces. In short, this can be a real threat to our businesses. Business is tough enough now. This could make us go down the drain.

I bit the bullet and wrote the attached letter to the commission. I'm sure you agree with what I told them.

I've also written this same letter to Country Cheeses and Rosewood Pharmacy. I suggest you talk to other businesspeople here whom you know well. We have to organize the merchants on this block and nearby to formally demand that the zoning commission withdraw this proposal.

Let's get together and talk. Right away, before this gets out of hand.

All the best,

Barbara Schwartz

Section Mistakes . . . Recover from an
10 Error That Could Lay You Low.

Gloss Over a Serious Blunder and Make a Fast Comeback from Potential Disaster.

Situation: You are a middle-management VP at a Wall Street financial power-house, McCool & Co., on a zoom track to the top, marked by your smart, effective stewardship of an important client, Largesse Data Processing. Now, you are sitting at your desk in shock, distraught and scared.

You were just informed of a high-visibility goof in an important and innovative financial plan you presented to this client. It underestimated the profit picture by 8 percent. While not fatal, it nevertheless was damaging and cast a dark shadow on the veracity of the entire presentation. To make matters worse, the client caught the error, and its marketing VP phoned you with the bitter news.

You see your brilliant reputation and sure-fire ascent to top management being shredded into tatters, your career eroding like a storm-ravaged beach. You must take hold and pull yourself together for rescue and rehabilitation. Operation Damage Control. NOW.

Strategy: Don't trivialize the error so as to seem uncaring.

Make it look like a small glitch. Stress that this was known before the client called, and it's been fixed. It won't affect results to any big extent. The program's viability is beyond question.

The schedule must continue as before, even accelerated for a fast-as-possible start. Once the program is in the works, it will create its own momentum, and the goof will soon be forgotten.

The glitch is the result of a supplier's error, but you, the team leader, accept responsibility. The buck stops here.

Massage the egos of the client's people. They'll enjoy personal accolades when this industry-shaking program is introduced.

Make corrections by tonight. Early tomorrow morning replace the tainted pages with corrected ones, at the client and internally.

You must come out looking good, even a hero, your top-seed reputation untarnished.

Deliver a letter to the client's marketing VP that buttresses this strategy tomorrow morning—all in a page and a half, single spaced—plus a short private P.S. to the same guy, on a separate page.

LETTER TO YOUR CLIENT

October 15, 1993

Mr. Gordon F. Chandler
Senior Vice President, Marketing
Largesse Data Processing, Inc.

_____

_____

Re: 11/12/93 Launch—Asset Marketing Program

Dear Gordon:

Sometimes two minds go into sync at about the same time. The day before you called me on the cost figure, we had been going through the process of double- and triple-checking all the numbers and found this glitch. We then revised the estimate, and I was within an hour of calling you when I got your ring.

You'll be glad to know, however, that we expect to come close to, or even hit, the profit we had previously projected because of savings in other parts of the program. As always, we've been conservative in our cost estimates and figured on the high side to allow a margin for contingencies.

Most importantly, Largesse is set to achieve—and may well exceed—the business and financial objectives you have established.

Additionally, this trailblazing program will further enhance, in a big way, Largesse's reputation as the industry's pacesetter. It will certainly reflect on the people who are involved in this program.

Gordon, just think how the entire financial community and the big players in information processing—not to say the investing public and the print and broadcast media—will sit up and take notice when this hits the public just four weeks from now. Our staff has been working around the clock to smooth along this launch date. All systems are in place; we'll start on schedule.

As an afterthought, everything is hush-hush here, and we're taking pains, as you are, to avoid any leaks. The PR gurus are starting to get the publicity juices flowing, so we expect a media blast a few days prior to the launch. Those in the media who, of necessity, have a hint of what will happen are keeping it under wraps.

Please be prepared for requests from the press and broadcast media titans for statements from you, your top management, and your associates. It would be good to have someone in your PR department keep it under control, and I'll work with you on this. Any media requests that come to us will be checked out with you, of course.

Best ever,

Michael M. Hemming

MMH/jr

Michael M. Hemming
Vice President

P.S. to Gordon

By the way, the cost glitch was the result of a misplaced figure by one of our suppliers, but, obviously, the responsibility rests with me.

The McCool people have the revised pages of the plan presentation and will be inserting them in all the copies at your offices. I'm sure that you and Largesse's management directors will be pleased.

Gordon, if you are available for lunch tomorrow, let's do it, and we can talk about implementing the details—the guts of which are neatly covered in the plan. Who does what and when. If not lunch, let's do this in the morning. I think we should also discuss setting up a meeting of our respective staffs.

M.M.H.

A Careless Miscue Makes You Look Bad. Make Light of It.

Two situations, two letters.

Situation I: You are a partner in an accounting firm. A report containing some financial information was supposed to be faxed to your client. Instead, it went to an unknown company because your secretary transposed two digits in the phone number incorrectly. The recipient was good enough to look up the correct number and relayed the fax to the right party. Fortunately, the information made no sense to the people who mistakenly received it.

Your client was incensed and expressed it with a loud and clear crescendo. They asked for an explanation.

Strategy I: How do you explain a dumb, careless error? There is no excuse. Try to toss it off without appearing to make light of it, and assure them it will never happen again.

From now on you have to check every fax, every letter, every message to this company. It's little things like this that could make you look stupid and alienate a client.

LETTER TO THE CFO

November 16, 1993

Mr. Charles Claypool
Vice President
Regent Technologies, Inc.

———————————————

cc: Ms. Jill Harrison, V.P. & Chief Financial Officer

Dear Chuck:

Thanks for letting us know about our error in dispatching a fax intended for you to another company we don't even know. It was unpardonable. It will never happen again.

It had private information, as you pointed out, something you don't want your competitors to know.

But, fortunately, the information was not really confidential. If it were, we obviously would not have sent it by fax. The people who got it and were good enough to look you up and call you had no inkling whatsoever of what it meant. It could have been a foreign language to them. Don't get me wrong. This is not an excuse.

One of our secretaries, who has been extremely reliable, transposed two of the digits in the phone number. It was human error combined with the unforeseen perils of technology.

Even though this hasn't caused any harm, we're by no means taking it lightly. Some day I'll tell you about the ugly repercussions around here, with my taking most of the beating because it was my letter. You know—the buck stops here.

Chuck, thank you for your understanding. It will not happen again. Of this you can be sure.

Best regards,

Situation II: You are in charge of a testing lab that is researching the efficacy of a weight reduction drug formulated by your client, a health systems company. You sent early top-line results, which has a bonehead ridiculous error. The figures for the test product and the placebo were reversed. It was caught the next day, and you have to report the correction.

Strategy II: No harm done. Thankfully, you caught the error before your client brought it to your attention. It could have been a cause célèbre with embarrassing implications if not discovered quickly.

Fax the correction right away, then mail the original. Give it a light touch. Have them smile instead of frown.

LETTER TO THE PRESIDENT

October 18, 1993   BY FAX

Dr. Michael Pryor
President
Leander Health Systems

_____

_____

Dear Mike:

There was a typo error in the figures we sent you yesterday morning on the top line G45 results. The results on the test panel and the placebo panel were reversed, and we caught it pretty quickly.

Here is the weight loss after the first 90 days of usage.

Average percent weight loss
After 30 days
Test   5.8%
Placebo   1.7

As you see, it looks like the new weight reduction formula is on the right track. According to the evidence so far, there are no adverse reactions of any consequence.

For some reason there is a smaller, although fairly significant, weight reduction with the placebo group at this early stage. This is likely a matter of the panel, early results, or halo effect.

Mike, when we first looked at the wrong figures we sent yesterday, we thought we had a wondrous new discovery in the placebo. We started to analyze what was in it. You've heard of great scientific breakthroughs from fortuitous accidents. No such luck here.

At any rate, it's good to give you this information. I'm sorry I can't report a new discovery. However, we can say that your test formulation is working well so far. Don't forget, however, that it's at an early stage.

Best wishes,

Excuse a Bad Error by Blaming Another Party (The Government in This Case).

Situation: You are the chief executive of a waste management company that has a choice contract with a large national construction company. In a waste cleanup at one of their sites, your office was careless about checking thoroughly with the EPA about environmental problems and special rules at this location. You okayed this operation, assuming from similar cleanup jobs that there was nothing to be concerned about.

Wrong! Your employees were two days into the work when the client's site manager said you were violating the rules. You checked and found he was correct.

You had to stop the work and regroup. Your men had to undo the damage before proceeding. It cost money, but luckily no summons was issued and no charges were filed. Think of the horror if the site manager hadn't told you. He informed his boss that you were about to cause an emergency, but he averted it with his good thinking.

Strategy: Your company, an outstanding name in waste management, is in a bad spot, and so are you—humbled and humiliated. There is no reasonable explanation. But you must try.

One excuse is to blame the government; most people have empathy with this. Even so, you must admit the mistake and note that you faced it, solved it, and saw to it that your client was not harmed. Here's more proof of the reliability of your company. You also have to give a nod of thanks to the site manager who saved you. Fortunately, you didn't lose a good customer. You might have.

LETTER TO YOUR CLIENT

October 21, 1993

Mr. Janusz Sowinski
Vice President
Harrison Construction Co.

_____

_____

Dear Mr. Sowinski:

What follows is an example of how hard it is at times to get proper information from the government, which is crucial in our business. The printed rules are often difficult to understand, even for experts in this industry such as us. Further, the regulations change and the interpretations change. This one certainly changed from what they told us, which is what we had been operating under.

It all boils down to the fact that what we told you about the EPA rule on the waste cleanup at your Stockton site was incorrect, even though we checked with their Washington office in advance and were assured of being in compliance with the regulations.

To his credit, your site manager informed us about it. I thanked him then, and I thank him now. I thank you for your understanding.

We have taken care of it. There is no harm done and no need to be concerned about any penalties or any bad reaction.

As I said, it's so difficult to make sure of regulation compliance, with the EPA as well as with so many other agencies. We are scrupulous about avoiding any problems, but an unintentional mistake can creep through.

It shows that even a dominant company in this industry can make a mistake when it comes to untangling the regulations of the government bureaucracies—federal, state, and local.

Fortunately, we have damage control procedures for this highly unlikely chance. We protect you against untoward circumstances that are not your doing, and this is what was important in this episode.

Best wishes,

A Customer Caught Your Overcharge and Now Questions Your Integrity. Plead Innocent.

Situation: You run a trucking company. A customer's credit allowance was misstated to your benefit. You knew it when it happened, but you were too busy putting out fires and figured you would get to it eventually. The customer caught it and raised a fuss. He indicated you were less than honest and threatened to dump you.

Strategy: Send a letter of sincere regret and repentance. Plead innocent. It's a computer mishap. Display embarrassment, chagrin, and outrage at your computer maestros who made the mistake, albeit an honest one.

It will never happen again. Your damage-doers have been chastised. Your information system is now error-proof. Guaranteed.

December 15, 1993

Mr. Jack Schultz
Warehouse Manager
Maritime Cargo Warehousing, Inc.

_____

_____

Dear Jack:

There's a lot to be said for computer technology and management information systems (MIS). But it sometimes replaces human error with computer error.

Yes, despite the up-to-date data-processing technology we have installed at enormous expense, sometimes errors occur. My technicians can tell you how this could happen. I can't really decipher all of their technical lingo.

Yes, it was a computer error that caused us to understate the value of your merchandise returns. To put it mildly, it's extremely embarrassing. I apologize for this mistake, and I'm sending you the amount we owe you. I raised hell with my technical people, and it won't happen again.

If it does, I'll double any money due you because of an error. I'm making this bet to show you how certain I am that from now on we will be error-free on your account.

All the best,

cc: Mr. John C. Aubrey, Jr.
     Comptroller

Climb up the Ladder . . . Improve Your Status, Move into the Leadership Elite.

A Rough, Tough New Group Took Over Your Company. They Don't See You Fitting In. Get Them to Accept You.

Situation: Your company, a giant food processor and marketer with traditional brands that are in almost every household pantry, merged into another dominant consumer products company.

The other side took over. Five of their top people, the new president and four of his cronies, are now running the combined operation—their way. They had a big hand in making the merger deal, with the help of financiers, bankers, lawyers, and accountants.

The new culture is a sea change from your former polite, staid surroundings. Now it is blood and guts. These guys are bold, brash, witty, and profane. They ridicule policies and rules and are certain of their invincibility.

Their great success so far is an enigma to you, except that they've been in the right place at the right time, where profits can't help but roll in handsomely and mistakes can be swept under the rug. They are superastute in the Byzantine arena of corporate politics. Nice guys, but rough and tumble.

You are the VP head of the Special Markets Division, responsible for nonretail sales. A tidy spot, and important, but out of touch with the glamour of the business.

Your patrician appearance and manner and your semi-British way of speaking, a product of your youthful upbringing in an area of eastern Canada, is a sorry handicap in this new environment.

They look on you as a plodding bureaucrat, a good behind-the-lines logistics officer. You may be necessary, but you won't storm any hills.

This new management clique drink together, eat together, stay out late together almost every night, and stroll in the next morning with a hangover and a laugh. They continually toss shoot-from-the-hip business ideas at each other. Some good, some fair, but mostly lousy. Their wives are good friends, too.

They golf together at a posh country club. The president, the leader of the pack, has an almost perfect swing and beats them quite consistently. He is on a first-name basis with various show-biz celebrities and golfs with a few of them.

Your new chief is riding a high road to glory as long as the business continues to thrive. His macho coterie is riding along with him. You want to ride behind. First of all, to secure your job. Secondly, to take even a baby step into the high road.

You are a consummate survivor. You are also smart. You'll find a way.

Strategy: Send the president a provocative memo—and c.c. the clique members. Display your brilliance. Tell them about the deals you made that are bringing wealth and stature to the company and how you've done it with boldness and panache. Give them a taste. Whet their appetites. Don't give the names of the famous companies and institutions you made deals with or any of the details. You must fire up their curiosity. Make them want to ask for more. Have them include you in their scheme of things.

Your writing has to be down-to-earth, brusque, pithy, and informal, in line with the life-style this group proudly flaunts.

You have to turn your image around. You are not a bland, ponderous, dull-as-crabgrass, back-room cipher. You are au courant, sharp, and audacious—like them.

IN-HOUSE MEMO TO THE HEAD OF THE NEW GROUP

September 15, 1993

To: Joseph Reynolds, President
         Harry Abelson
         Jim Harrigan
         Barry McIntyre
         Neil Peters

From: G. Carter Hedrick

Re: A Turn-on Message from the
         Guy in Charge of Special
         Markets

Being a veteran here (eight years), and as the head of the Special Markets Department, I want to give you an overview of what I've been doing—the deals that are in the works and those I have pending. I think you'll find them exciting.

It Will Get Your Creative Juices Flowing

I'm sure you will see ways in which you can fit these things into what your fertile minds are planning. By the way, it would help me to know what your plans are so that I can tilt my thinking (for future deals) to fit in with what you want to do.

I Need Your Ideas

Along these lines, it will be a big help to put my proposals and ideas up front for your finishing touches and your comments. Tell me which are lousy, which are great, which are strokes of genius, which are like an angel tapped my shoulder. It will be satisfying and pleasant to get this kind of input at last, sort of like sipping Johnnie Walker Black, neat.

Here's a Taste (No Pun Intended)

This is some of what I've been doing. I'll make it short and to the point. The complete descriptions, details, cost figures, and so on, are buttoned down in good-looking, bound reports.

Harvard Business School would be proud of the way it's done. You can read these reports anytime you want. I'll tell you now that all these programs are cost-effective and are good for our business or they wouldn't be around.

- Our Delightful Grains brand is now on the menu at school lunchrooms in eighty-three school districts in thirty markets, with a total population of forty-eight million, including ten million school kids.
  I'm working on getting this into more schools nationwide.
  Also, many of the kids are being given samples to take home.
  It was tough to crack this market, but we've done it.

- Tasty Bran and Macaroni n' Cheese are now on the meal trays of three *major* U.S. airlines and two foreign ones. We'll be getting more airlines soon as well as cruise ships.
- We've always done well with the hospital–nursing home trade, and our sales are getting heftier there. I have some great contacts, which solidify our position in this market with a good chance for further penetration.
- Think of this. The White House commissary is stocking six of our brands—so far. Yes, the president's White House in D.C. We can even flaunt this in our PR.
- We had to do a lot—like make food donations for flood and hurricane victims (tax deductible). We also sent three of our nutritionists into disaster areas.

I don't know why this hasn't been hyped to the media, but it may not be too late. It shows how we have sometimes not been able to exploit things to the maximum.

When Can We Get Together and Talk?

Now that you've gotten a nibble, how about letting your imagination feast at the banquet table? Give me direction so I can be side by side with what you have in mind on the overall scheme. I'm sure I can help with many of the things you are planning to do.

I'll drop by your offices.

Standing by,

G. Carter Hedrick

G. Carter Hedrick
VP, Special Markets

Break into the Power Epicenter.

Two situations, two strategies.

Situation I: Everyone in the company knows who the superstars are. The smart, sophisticated, articulate, witty, and charming few—the decision makers. They group together in their private circle, both at work and at play. They enjoy the glow of being at the center of power, knowing what's going on beyond the ken of the ordinary working stiffs. They are on the inside track of shaping their individual destinies.

You crave to get accepted into this policy-making elite. Outsiders are tolerated, even embraced occasionally, but are shunted away from the power center. It may take a deliberate yet disingenuous campaign to eventually break in—if you are worthy and the right material.

Strategy I: Do it slowly and choose the opportunity carefully. You see a start—a business plan that one of the power-core leaders produced. Throw bouquets at it and praise the author without seeming to kowtow.

You can't be obvious or odious. It may be an unobtrusive tiptoe toward your goal. In a very short memo, you must project cleverness, urbanity, sophistication—without affectation. Go for it.

November 19, 1993

To: Millicent Vandexter

From: Michael O'Hara

Dear Millicent:

I happened to see the document you put together—*Report and Plan of Action—Marketplace Development*.

Even though this topic is not in my specific province, and even at the risk of seeming to patronize you, I must make one point.

It is great, a matter of pride for the company. Of ultimate importance, the bottom line is that it will work.

Your piece brought to mind a sequel that might make sense. Sort of a lagniappe to this excellent plan. When you have some time, I'd like to share this thought with you to see what you think.

Millicent, you came up with a first-rate idea. Equally outstanding is your way of implementing it. You're great at transforming a concept into first-class action.

Regards,

[signature: Michael O'Hara]

Situation II: The ruling council at the organization where you work—a quasi-government entity to help our legislators bring government closer to the people—consists of polished individuals from prestige, big-name universities. The spawning grounds of the elite, the standard bearers in our society, the smooth leaders who make the ultimate decisions and issue the orders.

You, a product of lesser-known academe and of plain social background, are just as smart, just as ambitious, and just as able and qualified. Mission: Get into this elite club. Be one with the shapers of policy. You are convinced you have as much or more to offer as any of them.

Strategy II: Send a letter to the chairman of the association, the numero uno.

Bring to her attention that the fortunate people in the power circle seem to all have the same appearance, act the same, and have the same outlook in facing problems. A few came from humble beginnings but were assimilated into the ranks of the rulers. Having been at the top of the influence structure for many years, they are out of touch with the habits, hopes, and thinking of ordinary people, the vast 95 percent whom they lead.

Focus on your image of the common touch. You are as well educated, as sophisticated, and as smart as the ruling clique. And you know how to get to the heart and mind of Joe and Jo Citizen.

MEMO TO YOUR COMPANY CHAIRMAN

November 12, 1993

Mrs. Johanna Wilson
Chairman
Governmental Structuring Association
110 Connecticut Avenue
Washington, D.C.

Dear Mrs. Wilson:

As a GSA administrator in the Chicago office, may I make a suggestion that I know will put our organization closer to the public pulse and make us more effective in addressing people's needs? It should greatly stretch our ability to influence the vast heterogeneous public.

As can be readily seen, those in the ruling circle at our D.C. headquarters are products of pretty much the same privileges and educational backgrounds. Some came from advantaged families, others were born into humble households, but all have been out of touch for most of their adult lives with the common denominator of American families today.

How many had to take out second mortgages to make ends meet? How many had the dark rigor of having to find work when there was no work to be found? How many went without essentials in order to build a business? How many had to search for a loan when it meant survival and money was exceedingly tight? How many had to go to public clinics when their children were ill? Very few, if any, really.

All are brilliant scholars, truly. They received their education at elite power universities and then went on to the most acclaimed graduate schools.

Other people, and I include myself, of humble backgrounds, and with less prestigious but very creditable educational credentials, are out of the loop here. We have a tremendous handicap in getting into the top crust of this organization.

I say with deference, Mrs. Wilson, that we need more diversity in the selection of policy-making managers—diversity of family, work experience, and education, as well as gender, race, and age. This is what will make us more closely attuned to mainstream America.

Further, we, the not so fortunate, also want the challenge and the opportunity. We are also ambitious and capable.

Thank you so much for your time.

Respectfully,

There's a Spectacular Career-Boosting Opportunity That You Can Enter Only by Being Gentle and Humble. Do It.

Situation: You are a human resources associate at an aircraft manufacturer for the military and civilian markets. It's a junior executive job. An ad hoc corporate committee was set up at the request of the Defense Department to advise them on the conversion of military personnel skills to civilian uses. The purpose is to develop concrete proposals to help the Pentagon outplace inactivated military people.

   This is a great coup for the company. The PR drumbeaters have been hyping it for days. You must get involved. Even if it's in an unimportant way, even on the periphery, so long as your name can be identified with this project. It would be a spectacular entry on your résumé. Here is your big chance to stand out from the ordinary plodders in your next career move.

Strategy: Write to the committee chairman. Plead with him to get you into the loop, just so you can say you were part of this program. Tell him of your deep-rooted interest, your academic background in the subject, and how useful you can be. You are willing to help in any way, however menial, even if he chooses to use you for as little as a couple of hours a week.

   Imagine the distinguished people you'll be rubbing elbows with. Think of the important contacts you'll be making. Make it almost impossible to get a total refusal. When you are in, you can then look for ways to pirouette up the line to a meaningful position.

LETTER TO THE CHAIRMAN OF THE CIRCLE YOU WANT TO PENETRATE

September 21, 1993

Mr. Jeremy T. Legoe
Vice President
Kendor Aircraft Company

_____

_____

Re: Military Personnel
     Conversion Committee

Dear Mr. Legoe:

Please consider my exceptional background in the work your committee is committed to accomplish and my sincere interest in its mission.

Although my plate is quite full as a member of Kendor's Human Resources Department, I am eager to help, even after hours, if need be, because I know I can make a meaningful contribution.

My college courses in human resources included many hours of study in retraining and personnel allocation, and I've done original research in this subspecialty. My work at Kendor has received high ratings, and I continually upgrade my abilities through extensive reading.

Specifically, I would be useful in doing research, editing, correspondence, and in meeting and conference details. I am even willing to do secretarial or clerical work or however else you see fit to use me at this time.

Regardless of the amount of time I put in, even if it's as little as two hours a week, one thing is certain: You'll find me to be productive.

May we please meet to discuss this? I'll drop by your secretary's desk to find out when you will be available. All I ask is just a few minutes of your time.

                                        Very truly yours,

Your Boss Screwed Up. You Decide to Take the Heat. Now He Owes You One.

Situation: You are a marketing manager at a long-distance phone company. Your job is customer procurement, for which you conduct tie-in promotions with other companies.

Your boss, the VP of marketing, thought up an idea for a promotional offer on packages of high-turnover food products sold in supermarkets. He negotiated a deal with Happy Bakers for their popular-priced, widely distributed brand of cakes and cookies. He was head-high proud at having pulled this off. Top management were equally enthusiastic. Wow! We were getting into bed with a great consumer brand franchise.

Right from the beginning you had reservations about the kind of offer being made. Further, the people who buy Happy Bakers products are mainly blue-collar, middle and low income, which is not your market.

You told this to your boss, but he shut you up fast. You had to go along. Your job is to carry through on projects once they are approved. You can't be an unimaginative doomsayer. You psyched yourself into the companywide sweep of enthusiasm and dutifully carried out your assignment.

First, you did a test in two markets. The test had flaws in that it was difficult to segregate the baked goods distribution to two small areas. Results were okay, *maybe*, but not really conclusive. However, the optimistic fervor of the key executives caused them to be seen as good. The order from your boss was, let's go—now we roll out to the whole country.

This had to be done in stages because of Happy Bakers' distribution pattern. You are now in 30 percent of the country and moving ahead.

The promotion bombed. Badly. How do you spread this news? Who is to blame?

Strategy: If you let the chips fall as they deservedly should—that is, your boss made a deplorable judgment call—your boss will hate you. If you protect your boss from blame, even at your own expense, he'll love you. He'll protect you from harm now, and you can expect your just reward sometime later at a propitious time. You will have proved your loyalty to your boss.

You believe the latter option is the smarter thing to do. You send a memo to your boss about the sad news. You take the blame because you convinced him to do it, noting that the fault is yours.

Your boss will be able to show this memo to his management colleagues so they will know that his underling is the one who fell down. It will take the sting off him. Keep the documents handy that show your boss's faulty judgment, such as his directives to you, his flash of inspiration, asking for your input, etc.

Unless your boss has become insane, which isn't apparent, he is fully aware of the true story. Your devotion is inscribed, and he will respect you for shouldering the burden of responsibility in true executive style. He now owes you a reward or two sometime later.

September 8, 1993

To: Seth

From: Jason

I got more figures on our joint promotion with Happy Bakers. I'm sorry to report it hasn't changed for the better from last week.

> The downside . . . The response to our offer is continuing to decline. At this level of sales, we're losing money on every customer we get, even if they project out to a normal level of ongoing call volume. We're also losing money on store displays, flyers, etc.

> The upside . . . So far we only have exposure in 30 percent of the country. We can pull the plug now and stop the rollout before it goes any further.

Everyone was excited about this deal. They were sure it was going to be a winner. The two-market test we did showed good promise and gave us the signal to move ahead. But the rollout didn't live up to test indications.

I firmly recommend that we cut our losses. If you agree, I will inform Happy Bakers and the suppliers who are involved.

I'll have to take the responsibility on this. I handled it all the way. It was my baby. You sold it to management on the test results and on my assessment as well as my recommendation, which I believed was logical at the time.

The ball game isn't over. There will be more promotions this year. So far our batting average is good, even with this strikeout.

Jason

Going over Your Boss's Head for a Transfer and More Money.

Situation: Your immediate supervisor is very hard to work with. He's abusive and humiliates you if you don't adhere to his poorly stated instructions. Others have the same problem. He refuses to transfer you, and you haven't gotten a raise in two years.

You are ambitious; you want to move up and make more money. To do this, you feel you have to get out from under your boss and transfer to another division in the company. The company as a whole is a fine place to work, with good benefits and room for advancement.

Strategy: You have to go up the chain of command to the chief officer of the division.

You must get his attention and draw him to your problem with a respectful appeal to his sense of duty as overseer of all employees in his division. As such, he is responsible for efficiency and productivity, which involves good employee relations.

You can't appear to be insubordinate or a troublemaker. You must convince this top man of your loyalty to the company.

Don't make grave personal charges against your boss. You might be called upon to prove them, which could cause a problem and react against you. Nor should you involve others at this stage.

The chief will ask you to see him so that he can have more details. Tell him without censuring your boss, overtly diminishing his value to the company, or interjecting your personal feelings. Make sure it's credible, and keep it businesslike.

You don't want to be dismissed or have your future at the company compromised.

MEMO TO YOUR DIVISION CHIEF

January 11, 1994

To: Mr. Scott Pilney
        Vice President, Information Services
        Regency Data Processing, Inc.

From: Harriet Rosner

Dear Mr. Pilney:

I have been administrative assistant in the MIS section for the past three years. I have this need to write to you directly, which I believe you'll understand when you read further.

I greatly admire my supervisor, Mr. Ralph Jonas, for his technical competence and his dedication in carrying out his assignments. However, I find him very difficult to work for, with the result that I'm not able to perform to my potential. This has become intolerable and is causing me a great deal of anguish.

I made a formal request to Mr. Jonas for a transfer to another department, which he refused to sanction. Further, I haven't received a raise in two years.

I am very conscientious. I know my duties well, and I want to do the best possible job for Regency Data Processing. But I'm in a stressful situation with apparently no chance of advancement.

May I please ask that you consider my request for a transfer so that I can better exercise my abilities. All I ask for is this opportunity. I'm proud and happy to be working for Regency, and I want to make this company my career. It's my goal to do well here.

You should know that I am writing this on my own and do not suggest that this troubling situation may occur with other people in my department.

Thank you so much, Mr. Pilney, and please understand my need to contact you directly. As you see, I have no choice.

                                        Respectfully yours,

                                        Harriet Rosner

Section 12 Get Your Troops in Line. Inspire Productive Thinking.

Make Pragmatic Sense out of Voluminous Data, and Change Debate into Doing.

Situation: You are the top guy responsible for marketing policy at a durable goods manufacturer, a worldwide behemoth. You commissioned a market research company to conduct a consumer survey in order to get helpful information for marketing and advertising planning. The research report is a detailed 258-page document with tables, charts, and graphs—a voluminous compilation of data tabulated by groups, subgroups, with regressions and digressions.

You asked your marketing personnel to analyze the study for the purpose of determining what to do about it. Numerous recommendations emerged from their reports, some exceptional, some good, some abstruse, some impractical, some narrowly focused, all reflecting a host of conflicting viewpoints.

Strategy: You have to get the ship on an even keel, sailing ahead on a steady course. Send a memo to all your marketing division heads. Zero in on the nitty-gritty findings without going into nonessential detail.

This means taking 258 pages of complex data and transforming them into a practical couple of pages. It's the starting point for getting the salient research findings out of binders and into the real world.

You want to arrive at a total marketing strategy that is effective and makes sense. You note that further cogent comments are welcome, but positive action has to start in one month.

IN-HOUSE MEMO TO YOUR ENTIRE STAFF

February 11, 1994

To: All Marketing Supervisors and Advertising Managers

From: Betty Freeman

Re: Consumer Research Survey—on the Opinions of Consolidated Electronics Corp., Its Products, and Its Advertising

We've all had a chance to digest this expensive 258-page survey and get some nourishment out of it. By the way, it's a very good study. It could be incredibly good if used properly.

I made an aggressive assault on this document, piercing through every finding. I also studied everyone's comments, written and oral. There were many opinions and many conflicting interpretations. If we followed everybody's recommendations, it would take many years and an inestimable amount of money.

Unlike the federal government, we cannot sustain a policy of "Try it, see if it works. If not, try something else." Also, unlike the federal government, we cannot operate at a deficit for long.

After sifting through all that I mentioned, I've zeroed in on a number of bedrock findings on which we can build a plan of action:

- Everybody we care about knows of our company.

- Most have a good opinion of us. A fairly significant minority have a less-than-good or poor opinion. Enough so that we should do something about it. The study tells the reasons—for example, what these people are thinking. We should keep these negatives in mind in all our consumer communications venues.

- Our products are liked by almost everyone who is familiar with them. High numbers rate them "superior." This should be the case, considering all the measures we take to assure high quality and the links we set up with customers for the fast redressing of grievances. We must keep up what we're doing in this regard.

- Our pricing is considered fair.

- Our advertising is remembered by more than half of consumers but few remember our slogan. Not too bad, but not great, either.

What I got out of all this is that we do a good job producing products, pricing them well, and giving good customer service. We could do a better job of reinforcing these facts and building on this positive image with the public. And, by the way, with the trade.

Let anyone who has anything cogent to add please do so. Study the research report again. We have to arrive at a common agreement on what to do, what to tell our ad and PR agencies, our employees, service sector, and so on.

Let's have agreement on all this in four weeks, which is March 11. On this date, we'll have our first action meeting—the most important one, because it will ignite the engines to roll our new strategy down the runway for takeoff.

I know we'll go into this in a spirit of cooperation to do what's best, but occasionally some people get carried away. I suggest these rules:

> No gridlock
> No defensive postures
> No adversarial overtones
> No contentious expressions or thoughts
> No self-serving statements
> No focusing on a problem without a
>   contravening solution
> No eulogizing of previous strategies
> No gratuitous praise or criticism
> No wasted motion
> No wishful thinking

When our whole program is in place, it will be enshrined on stone tablets and all will bow in reverence.

Have a great weekend,

Get Through Abstractions and Right to the One Salient Point.

Situation: You are the head of a well-recognized architectural firm. Profits took a dive, meaning trouble. You must get your employees on track in order to change minus earnings to plus.

Strategy: Your staff has to understand a fundamental conviction, namely, that you are in business to make money in order to pay bills and have some left over. They have to set their thinking straight on getting the business back on track. You asked your staff architects to write you a memo with the answer to the bedrock question: "What are we in business for?" See what they have to say, and then get back to them.

IN-HOUSE MEMO TO YOUR PROFESSIONAL STAFF

February 11, 1994

To: Jake Davidoff
      Lindsey Anderson
      Diane Quester
      Lars Stenveld

From: Seth Herman

I asked you to specify what this architectural company is in business for. What is our cardinal purpose?

I don't have to tell you this is to address the basic thing we are supposed to do—a first step in overcoming the big slide in profits the last three quarters and get us onto a growth curve.

The answers I've seen are . . .

   Design outstanding structures we can be proud of.

   Get new standards of construction integrity.

   Lead our clients to innovative and greater architectural achievements.

These are all nice, but no one gave the right answer, which is our hard-core objective, our unalterable responsibility that's ahead of anything else.

This is it. We are in business to make money. The other words of wisdom are directly relevant, no doubt, but they are not the bedrock reason for our being here. It's profits that make for these nice offices and the perks we enjoy as well as pay our salaries. Their absence will cause cessation of same.

Let's keep this in mind as number one.

                              Have a great day,

                              Seth Herman

Restoring Worker Morale after a Firing Bloodbath.

Situation: Your company had a severe downsizing, caused by two years of plummeting earnings. Twenty-five percent of the employees have been pink-slipped. You have to keep a charge-ahead attitude in the sales department, which you head up. You cannot afford a downcast demeanor. Your salespeople have to be upbeat and optimistic in explaining the new company structure to their customers.

Strategy: Send a memo to your division managers, with instructions to distribute it to their troops. Tell them that things are fine and that business will be moving ahead at a much better pace because of greater efficiencies now in force. Everyone now here is secure, with a chance to make more money and to move up the ladder faster.

October 18, 1993

To: Joe Durso
        Felice D'Amico
        Bernie Bronsweig
        Carol Bloom
        John Farley

From: Harry Medina

Re: Reorganization of the Sales Department—the Facts.

Q. Why did we make this move?

A. At times we fell over each other, causing problems with our accounts. There were instances when two of our salespeople contacted the same customer. It was necessary to have a more orderly sales structure.

Q. Why were so many people laid off?

A. We had a lot more people than necessary for the volume of our business, especially in light of the new technology we installed in the last couple of years, which in itself would entail a work force reduction. This streamlining will allow for more individual opportunity. And, insofar as the sales department is concerned, there will be more commissions for those who are here now.

Q. Will there be any more layoffs?

A. I can't forecast the future, but the answer at this time is no. The reorganization is complete. No more layoffs are contemplated. Everyone here is important. There is a new opportunity now to stay and thrive, which we want all of you to take advantage of.

Q. How is business right now?

A. Very good. There are fewer sales now, but they are more profitable because of the efficiencies we put into place. Business looks like it's growing. We're happy. You should be, too.

Q. What changes are going on in our information processing?

A. Our computer programming was falling behind the new technology. We are now getting data faster and more in tune with the marketplace.

Q. Will more people be hired later on?

A. Yes, as the business grows and it gets too much to handle for you guys. We'll let you know what goes on. The people on board now will get the first crack at the best positions and promotions.

This should dispel the rumors and put us on track. And every one of you, please let me know if there is anything else on your mind that you want answered.

My thanks to you all; I'm convinced we have the best sales force in the business. So does our chairman and president.

Best wishes,

Larry Medina

P.S. Please distribute copies of this to all the people in your divisions. I want them to know as much as you do.

Praise a Winning Accomplishment by Your Colleagues, but Curb Complacency.

Situation: You are an ad agency VP account supervisor on the shop's biggest account, a world-renowned toiletries company. Your creative people have been in a strenuous and stressful exercise on a new TV commercial for your client's shampoo brand.

    The advertising theme is a new creative idea. The commercial, in preproduction format, has gone through extensive testing among consumer panels along with commercials from two other agencies that are trying to get this business.

    Hooray! Yours came out on top.

Strategy: Get the good news out to the creative team quickly in an interoffice memo, heaping praise on the people directly responsible. Copies go to all the key people, including the agency's chairman and president.

    Without taking the edge off their pride of accomplishment, you have to point out that the job is far from over and that there's much more to do to get this commercial on the air. You don't want them to wallow in a euphoric glow when there is so much work ahead. Give the memo a smile to take the edge off your pushing them back to the workbench.

    You will have solidified their loyalty and inspired a continued effort. You will demonstrate that this is the kind of wide recognition everyone in the agency can expect when they do a good job.

IN-HOUSE MEMO TO ALL WHO PARTICIPATED IN THE WINNING ENDEAVOR

October 1, 1993

To: Candy Steinman
         Norm Sanchez
         Penelope Durgin
         Steffi Smith
         and others who had a hand in Commercial TF103

From: Sandy Warfield

You produced a winner. It sure makes everyone here look good.

The client just gave me the results of the three commercials tested. Yours came out on top. I always knew it was great advertising, but it's nice to have it confirmed. Best of all, the client is delighted with it, supremely so. So are we.

Before you decide to take the rest of the day off or go into a euphoric glaze, think of what has to be done.

    1. First, walk around a bit, greet your friends; praise each other. Then sit down and look out the window for five minutes or so.

    2. Take a long lunch. (1½ hours.)

    3. Later this afternoon, start getting ready for production. Casting, sets, studio, location, etc., and figure out the final budget.

    4. All of this has to be client approved by October 22. Sooner is better, because it must be on the air in March.

    5. Other assignments will be coming up, starting a few days from now. I'm sure you'll take these new creative challenges in your usual masterful strides.

    6. Have a nice weekend.

Be especially proud in that we beat out two other top agencies. Congratulations to everyone!

Admiringly,

Sandy

cc: Sigmund Brandberg, Chairman
       Theodora Ramos, President
       The Staff

Admonishing the New Business Pitch Team After a Costly Defeat. It Should Have Been a Victory.

Situation: The new business team at the marketing communications agency you preside over is generally composed of five or six of the star performers. It is an ad hoc group that is selected for each presentation. They pull together and deliver the presentation, drawing on other staff members for specialized input.

One such team made a costly endeavor for a juicy account plum that had two other agencies also reaching for it. Your group wasn't successful, even though you consider them more talented than the winning agency's team.

They didn't prepare as well. They were also overconfident. They knew they were good, and they knew they had superlative ideas to show off. But their ideas weren't spelled out convincingly. All of this added up to losing instead of winning.

Strategy: Send them a group memo. Bring them to reality as to what makes a successful new business team. Point out their foibles, what they did wrong, and what they didn't do right. Tear them apart and then brace them up for the next new business encounter.

IN-HOUSE MEMO TO THE TEAM MEMBERS

April 8, 1993

To: The Performers Who Made the Presentation
For the Sugarland Account.
Rowena Balterman
Casper Winters
Mary Beth Innis
Gene Koenig

From: Barbara Thomas

One Step Back . . . Let's Make It Two Steps Forward Next Time.

I don't have to tell you that Will, Ruby & Partners aren't as good as we are. So how come they beat us out on the Sugarland business?

We had wonderful ideas to show Sugarland. We were confident. We had a good attitude. We were the best team in the tournament. We didn't score the winning run. Why?

We would have won . . . IF . . .

IF we had spent more time at Sugarland in order to learn more about their business. We thought we knew it. But we didn't know it well enough. We were badly out of sync on one of our suggestions. It hurt our image.

IF we had consulted with the trade press to find out what the competition was doing. One of our gold-plated ideas had recently been done by a competitor. That was a major embarrassment.

IF we had given ourselves more time to thoroughly check our write-up. Some of the typos made us look small-time.

IF we weren't so damn cocky. Some of our shoot-from-the-hip answers were evasive, one was double-talk, and one was plain wrong.

Every championship team and every superstar must train constantly and be in top condition. They have to be thoroughly prepared for every single game, mentally and physically.

Repeat: thoroughly prepared.

Talent alone does not win. A lot of behind-the-scenes hard work is an absolute necessity. That's what makes a winning team. That's what brings in big salaries.

We learned a lesson. A costly one. Did you add up the cost of this presentation? You'll be shocked.

Let's make sure we're ready when the next one comes up. B.T.

You Must Lift Morale After a Failure.

Situation I: *Lost a Political Election*

Your friend was her party's choice to run for the state legislature. She was an administrator in a state regulatory board and had never run for an elective office before. You are head of a media-consulting company and worked full-time on her campaign, including the fund-raising effort.

It was lot of time, a lot of money, and a bitter campaign. She lost in a close vote, 48 percent to 52 percent.

Your friend is an excellent choice for public office: brilliant, honest, idealistic, and dedicated. She must keep trying. Encourage her.

You want to continue working with her with a view to preparing for her next campaign—and the next, and the next. She will have a long public career if she has good advisers and fund-raisers.

Strategy I: Send a personal letter to her home, with copies to all the party bigwigs. Boost her morale. Encourage, even beseech her, to remain active in politics. This is just one episode in what will be a successful public service career.

LETTER TO A CANDIDATE WHO LOST A
POLITICAL ELECTION

November 10, 1993

Ms. Lucille Degrandi

_____

_____

Dear Lu:

Winston Churchill remarked that the most important quality for success is the ability to overcome failure.

What resounding failures Churchill experienced in his public career! And what stunning successes! Success couldn't have come if he hadn't risen from cataclysmic downfalls.

Many other historical figures have also had to rise from the ashes, dust themselves off, and go on to victory and fame. It took fortitude, dedication, and guts. It took greatness.

You are great, Lu. You have incredible ideas, ideas that will inspire our state and our country. The party needs you.

This is a temporary lull in your road to the top. We want you to keep at it, undaunted. You are too good to take a back seat.

There will be other elections. Bigger fields of endeavor. Bigger challenges to triumph over. Keep at it, Lu, and you will win. We are behind you, more than ever. I am honored to be at your side.

With admiration and loyalty,

Situation II: *Failed to Get a New Business Gem*

You are the senior marketing VP of a long-distance phone company. You formed a company team of several energetic marketing people to go after a juicy piece of corporate business. An all-out effort was put into it, with pressure-driven, crazy-long hours, but a competing company won.

Strategy II: Hoist up the team's morale and their pride. They didn't win, but they didn't lose either. They truly showed themselves to be big-leaguers. They have to be recharged for the next spare-no-effort push for new business.

IN-HOUSE MEMO TO THE TEAM THAT FAILED TO GET A NEW BUSINESS GEM

November 10, 1993

To: The Consummate New-Business Team
 Jenny Robinson
 Kate Carmody
 Bernie Schwab
 Mac Simon

From: Bill Palmer

Dear Team:

We didn't win the Hero Automobile account that we worked so hard to get, but we came out winners nevertheless.

ATD managed to snatch the brass ring this time. I want to tell you now, before you see it in the papers.

This doesn't mean they had the best presentation. We had the best. But the politics and vagaries of the battle don't always raise the hand of the best.

Everybody here is proud of the big-league presentation we put together and how you guys did it. It was excellent, and still is. It's good enough to show off with pride to anyone. Let's clear the decks for the next big one.

With much thanks,

Bill Palmer

P.S.   We can dust this presentation off to go after another car account.

Get Your Staff—and Your Vendor—Firmly into Line, While Not Ruffling Egos.

Two letters:

"Correct" your vendor.

"Correct" your staff.

Situation: You are the director of marketing communications of a top packaged-goods toiletries manufacturer. The executive-level supervisors are the youthful cream of the crop from top MBA schools. They are clever, eager, and often oblivious to rules and procedures that may slow their drive for recognition and riches.

Each one wants to be the first to get data from your consumer research supplier, sometimes even before it is assembled, so that they can present it to upper management with their intelligent comments. Being the first with inside information brings attention and kudos.

This helter-skelter drive to be the bearer of tidings causes confusion, mistakes, and misguided analyses. It makes you look bad. It causes your department to be perceived as disorganized and leaderless.

Strategy: Send a letter to the head of the research company saying that all information they gather—every little piece of it—is to come to you first. They must not comply with individual requests from your staff. Point out the reason and that the former confusion was not his people's fault. They were taking orders from a client, yes, but from the wrong staff member. Only you represent the client.

Then send a memo to your staff, with a copy of the letter you sent to the market research company. Specify the new dictum. Enlist their support and praise them for their intelligence, their striving to excel, and the wonderful job they are doing.

LETTER TO THE VENDOR

January 18, 1994

Mr. Anthony DiLoresta
President
Target Marketing Research

_____

_____

Subject: The Transmitting of Information

Dear Tony:

I very much appreciate the consumer data you are bringing to light.

But there is a problem in how you transmit the information to us. It affects our judgment on what to do with it, which in turn affects our decision-making process. This, in turn, affects the value of the information you gather.

Here's the chain of command in your dealings with this company:

1. All your data—reports, top-line, bottom-line, objective, subjective, interpretive, inferential, or whatever, phoned or written—comes to me first. No other copies are to go to anybody.

2. This office will look it over and discuss it with you or whomever you may designate. I will then review it with the appropriate people here. We'll then come to a judgment as to how to handle it.

3. I or one of my staff may then ask you to send along multiple copies of one or more of your reports. That is, your own data and analysis, which is not to include any interpretation by anyone outside your office.

We are pretty much a freewheeling organization peopled by smart young turks who work hard and accomplish a lot. It's great for this company.

They have often called you for top-line data or early results—even before they are fully compiled. They asked to see reports, or Target's interpretation, before they are formally prepared. Several received reports before anyone else here. You complied with their requests. It's not your company's fault. You answered a client's requests.

It has, however, gotten out of hand. It is bad business procedure, and it's going to stop. From this time on!

If anyone at your place gets such a request from anyone here without my approval, they are to refer the person to the statements in this letter and then inform me.

I'm sure, Tony, that you are in accord with what I'm saying. I'm also certain you are happy to see it changed. Keep up the good work.

Best regards,

P.S.   My staff has seen a copy of this letter.

IN-HOUSE MEMO TO YOUR STAFF

March 3, 1993

To: Shelley Bogart
        Oscar Fogarty
        Nancy Hanna
        Bud Kingman
        Linda Miranda

From: Betty Jo Anderson

Attached is a letter I sent yesterday to Tony DiLoresta of Target Research. Read it before starting on the rest of this memo.

Now that you've read the attached, here are my comments to all of you.

First of all, I'm proud of the superb job you are doing. You handle it with intelligence, verve, and an insatiable eagerness to excel. It's good for this company. In fact, it's great.

Now for the sticky rules that you see in my letter to Tony. It may confine your exuberance, but it increases your effectiveness and your value to this department and the company.

We have to be a team. Let's each have the advantage of the others' judgments. This is not to say everything has to be dictated by consensus. But we must have collegiality. There is a huge advantage to having the combined wisdom of several brilliant minds in reviewing a problem.

At the same time we should take into account what a very clever guy, Henry L. Doherty, once said: "Some of our problems can no more be solved by majority opinion than a problem in arithmetic."

The bottom line on marketing research:

> All reports, comments, results, judgments, opinions, and surmises must come from my office. The positive input of each of you will be fed into what is distributed to the other people here, with full credit given.

> You will have better recognition of your good thinking than before. What's more, you won't be caught giving premature or partial results, which can be, and often are, misleading. Be happy.

I'm glad you are here,

Betty Jo

Get Rid of a Problem Assistant with a Smoke Screen of Magnanimity.

Situation: You are a division chief in a data communications company heading up their business networks department. Your assistant is brilliant, resourceful, ambitious, and headstrong, not to mention impatient in scurrying up the ladder.

He upstages you in meetings as a tacit demonstration of his superior abilities. Cunningly, he avoids any outward indication of disloyalty. He even puts on a display of die-hard allegiance.

Simply put, he is a threat to your job. You have to get rid of him. But how do you do it to someone who is bright, gifted, hardworking, and has made everyone aware of the superb job he is doing? The rest of the staff consider you lucky to have him working for you.

Strategy: *Voila!* A job opened up in another department. It's a nice step up from your deputy's current rank. A good promotion for him.

Recommend him for the position. You hate to lose him, but why hold a good man down? Management should give him a break. He earned it. This clearly unselfish gesture for the corporate good demonstrates to all your outstanding executive posture.

You won't be left in the lurch. You already have a replacement on tap.

IN-HOUSE MEMO TO YOUR DEPARTMENT HEAD

December 16, 1993

To: Mr. Frank DiClemente
        Vice President, Marketing and Planning
        PCI Data Networks Inc.

From: Ted Zimmermann

Let's not hold a good person down.

I'm talking about my assistant, Tony Rivers. It regards the position that is open as new products manager.

Tony has been doing a great job for me, as we all know, and I would really hate to lose him. But he is ready for an upward move, and I know he yearns for it.

It would be good for the company to give Tony a chance to prove himself in this spot, and I'm confident he'll make it. It goes without saying that we have to move our good people along and up when an opportunity arises.

It would ordinarily be tough for me to find a replacement. However, I have someone in mind who is ready and able. I'm sure he'll be able to fill Tony's shoes with no lost motion.

Why not give Tony a break when he is ready for it? And importantly, when he has earned it?

Ted Zimmermann

You Have to Fire the Relative of an Important Client.

Situation: The exec VP of one of your big-time clients asked if you would give his nephew a job in your company, a large food wholesaler. You put the lad to work in client and customer relations. He is capable, but nowhere near a world-beater, and you cannot have him take on more responsibilities without upsetting other more deserving people.

He has to be let go, but very, very carefully so as not to make waves with his uncle.

Strategy: Send a private memo to him in which you laud his performance and note that letting him go is intended to further his career advancement. You'll try to help him find another spot that will be more suitable for his talents and ambition.

You can be sure he will show your memo to his uncle.

IN-HOUSE MEMO TO THE PERSON BEING DISMISSED

January 11, 1994   PRIVATE AND CONFIDENTIAL

To: Jim Ambrose

From: G. Clark Walker

This won't make you feel good now, but in the long run you'll look back and be very happy I did it.

As you can see when you look around, we're reorganizing our entire staff. What it comes to is that there is really no room for advancement for people at your level. The people above you are well ensconced, and they are at an age where they'll be around here many years.

Jim, you're too good a guy, too talented, too smart, and have too much potential to be locked into a static position like this.

We really hate to lose you. But we want you to be in a place where you can now start to blossom. Your next move should be a bigger job than you have here. Look on this as an opportunity for career development.

You have the run of all the facilities here if necessary—your office, the phone service, typing help, and so on. We'll do all we can to help you connect with the right spot. I personally will get in touch with friends in the business.

This is a nudge to help you to bigger and better things. The timing is now, when you are ready for it. Stay here as long as necessary in finding a spot. It's important that you pick your new post carefully. Let's get together and talk. Give me a call.

Best wishes,

G. Clark Walker

Firing a Vendor Without Incurring Ill Will.

Situation: You are a principal at a car rental franchise. You hired two sales representative companies for commercial accounts. One of these is incurring higher expenses (which are billable to you) than the others, but their sales aren't any better. Your overall business slowed down lately, which requires one of these reps to be let go. The finger points to the least productive one.

Strategy: It's a fine, reputable company, with good resources, and their people have contributed good thinking on your commercial business. You don't want any bad feelings, and you want to maintain friendly relations. There may be a need to call on them in the future. Express these thoughts in a letter and follow up by phone.

LETTER TO THE VENDOR

March 15, 1993

Ms. Kathy Loughran
National Sales Manager
AGA Sales Representatives

———————————————
———————————————

Dear Kathy:

I'm sure you realize that the the amount of orders we've been getting from AGA in relation to expenses has caused us to review our relationship. We are, regrettably, obliged to terminate our association.

I say regrettably because you and your staff have been so helpful in developing our sales strategy. The currently slow sales activity is certainly not the fault of the AGA staff on our account. We're continuing with our other representative on a basis that I believe may not be practical for AGA at the present flow of business.

We certainly hope the time will come when we can call on you again. Our people have often spoken about you and your staff's professionalism and business judgment. You have a lot of admirers here.

You may be less one customer (not as profitable as it had been), but you retained a large number of friends and solid boosters.

I'm looking forward to working with you again.

Best regards,

Have the Account Executive on Your Account Replaced Without Hurting Him.

Situation: You head a marketing group at a long-distance phone company. The account executive at your ad agency is not quite up to snuff in handling your needs. He's short of being a super performer, thus not quite the kind of person you want. The agency is top-notch, and you believe you could get better work out of them if someone more capable handled your account.

    You want him replaced. However, he happens to be a nice guy. You have a rapport, and you don't want to hurt him. Above all, you don't want him to lose his job.

Strategy: You must state your wish to the group head the account man reports to. It would be too harsh to spring it on the phone; your intent might be misunderstood. A letter followed by a phone call is the least harmful way.

    The letter should salute the agency's work and praise the account executive. Give a convincing reason for the need to change without stigmatizing him. Why hurt him? Why cause bad feelings? Why not make everyone happy?

LETTER TO THE ACCOUNT EXECUTIVE'S BOSS

January 14, 1994

Ms. Leonore Schram
Executive Vice President
Arrow Advertising Inc.

_____

_____

Dear Leonore:

This is a thank-you note, well deserved. At the same time, I'm taking this opportunity to make a request. Well, not so much a request as throwing out a suggestion for you to consider.

The staff on our account has been doing a remarkable job, sometimes under tough conditions. I want you to know firsthand how we feel about it. Jeff has spearheaded the group in a first-rate, professional manner. You supported him when he needed it.

I thank you, and I thank Jeff.

Now for the request—rather suggestion—that I don't want misunderstood. You see, we have a policy here of rotating personnel. It's a way of making sure that an individual doesn't get into rigid habits in handling any particular segment of our business. It brings a more diversified talent stream into the problem-solving complex. I think this is good management. I'm sure you do, too.

Jeff has been the lead person on our account for two years now. And he's very good. We all like him, and we will hate to lose him. But I think the time has come for a change of command. It's done in the military for good reason. For the same reason, it's good in business.

Please explain this to Jeff. I will too. Naturally, we want him to be close at hand to guide the new person, especially at the beginning. His acute sense of our business is invaluable.

Let's talk about this, Leonore. Naturally, I'll want to see Jeff's replacement before there is an official assignment.

Best wishes,

Uplift the Spirits of One of Your Employees After You Promoted His Assistant to Be His New Boss.

Situation: Your VP of purchasing left for another job, and you have to fill the spot in a hurry. A logical choice is the purchasing manager, Stan. He's been with the company for twenty-four years. He is dedicated, honest, reliable, and knows his job from A to Z. But he is not quite officer material. You want an executive-style individual, one with fresher thinking.

Stan's assistant is sharp, youthful, college-educated, and has been well groomed by Stan for an upward move. She can handle the VP position for less money than you would have to pay an outsider. What you save will allow you to give Stan a "feel-good" raise and still come out ahead. He is due for a raise anyway in about three months.

How do you handle Stan?

Strategy: Send Stan a personal note telling him how well he is thought of and the wonderful job he's doing. Thank him for taking his assistant under his wing and teaching her the ropes so that she is now ready for an upward move.

This is no reflection on Stan. Being in this new spot would bore him. Besides, the money isn't much more than what he's making. He is being considered for more interesting things, both inside and outside of purchasing.

Stan will see a 4 percent raise next payday.

On a personal level, ask him to relate your best wishes to his wife and kids.

IN-HOUSE MEMO TO THE EMPLOYEE

October 22, 1993

To: Stan Weinberg

From: Otto Stritch

Stan, you may have heard rumors, but I want to personally tell you that Greta Nielsen is being promoted to VP purchasing starting November 16.

I also want to take this opportunity to tell you how much we appreciate the extraordinary way you do your job and that it hasn't gone unnoticed. Furthermore, your marvelous tutelage of Greta and your bringing her along to more and more responsibilities made it possible for her to be selected for this spot. You will have a good friend there.

You are probably wondering why you didn't get the position.

Stan, you've spent so many years in purchasing that moving a notch higher would mean no new challenge for you. You would be doing the same thing, only under more pressure. There is little difference in pay. We have you in mind for other important assignments both within and outside the purchasing department.

Financially, you'll be doing well too. You've been here a long time and have accumulated a nice retirement egg. And you can expect a 4 percent raise in your next paycheck as an expression of our appreciation of your work.

I know you'll cooperate with Greta all the way in this transition.

Please give my best wishes to Ethel and your children, Peter and Mary.

With best wishes,

Otto Stritch

You Were Hired on a Sincere (?) Handshake, and Pushed Aside at the Last Minute for Someone Else.

Two situations:

 I. You have a job and were going to switch.

 II. You are unemployed and are looking.

Situation I: A headhunter tapped you, a civil engineer, for a promising career jump at a well-known engineering firm. It means leaving the somewhat smaller establishment where you now work.

You had a right to assume the deal was final. The senior engineers promised that the job was yours. They said a written statement noting job responsibilities, salary, and so on, was on the way.

Out of the blue, they had a change of mind. Another engineer got the job. You were informed quite hastily, six business days after their solemn verbal "commitment."

Strategy I: Why be timid and let it slide by, chalking it up to the fortunes of the marketplace? You went through a complex network of scrutiny, hand-holding, negotiating, and staying awake nights conjecturing the move in your mind. You and your family had become psyched up about your new status.

You had started going-away preparations at your present shop. Fortunately, senior management wasn't officially notified, although you discreetly passed along the news to a couple of your associates. You feel humiliated.

Your dignity and professional credibility, not to mention your own sense of self-worth, call for not taking it lying down. You can't change the company's last-minute decision, but send them a letter stating the discomfiture, indeed the harm, this has caused you. The indication is that considering the way they conducted themselves, you don't want the job anyway.

LETTER I: YOU HAVE A JOB AND WERE GOING TO SWITCH

April 11, 1994

Mr. Howard C. Ross
Executive Vice President
Gatley & Rogers Engineering Associates, Ltd.

_____

_____

Copy: Betty Ann Schomer,
        Dean & Sherwood,
        Personnel Consultants

Dear Howard:

Being left at the altar has put me in an embarrassing fix.

By no means am I suggesting that you reverse your decision, nor am I even questioning it. The fact is, in view of what has happened, I do not want the position. This letter is merely intended to point out the harm your sudden shift caused me.

I accepted your verbal commitment in good faith, in advance, as you put it, of a written hiring agreement. You told me to report three weeks hence.

Since you wanted me to start in this short time, I had to immediately make preparations for terminating my current job. This meant hurrying up my work load, shifting responsibilities to others, and so on. And I couldn't avoid indicating the move to some of my colleagues and my immediate supervisor. You have caused me much embarrassment.

I should add that Sanders & Stevens are most happy to have me remain here.

In the interest of your company's reputation, I am due a better apology than I was given on the phone by your associate.

Very truly yours,

Situation II: You are a professional civil engineer, out of work because of a business reversal at your former employer. Economic conditions bode ill for out-of-work civil engineers. Finding a job is a gloomy prospect.

A headhunter put you in touch with a wonderful opening at a well-known firm. There were intense meetings and get-to-know-you sessions, and you came out on top (for a few days, that is). Actually, they told you, with much praise, that the job was yours. You were to start in two weeks.

You and your family were euphoric. Then, five days later, like the Chernobyl blast, your world was shattered. They told you it was off. Someone else they had previously negotiated with agreed to accept the job. You are back to a desperate square one.

Strategy II: Send a letter noting that you had good reason to conclude that you had been hired. The serious discussions you had during the past two months precluded you from actively pursuing other opportunities.

Make them feel guilty, but be gracious. You are in no position to show pique; what's more, it won't do you any good. Why not keep up a positive relationship? It's silly to burn bridges. They may keep you in mind for something else later on.

LETTER II: YOU ARE UNEMPLOYED AND ARE LOOKING

February 11, 1994

Mr. Howard C. Ross
Executive Vice President
Gatley & Rogers Engineering Associates, Ltd.
_____
_____

Dear Howard:

I must say it was a sudden jolt getting the news, so soon after your verbal commitment. I guess things like this sometimes happen.

It set me back quite a bit, because I had informed another company that was interested in me that I was no longer available. Furthermore, during the two months in which we held meetings and negotiations, it was difficult for me to pursue other opportunities.

At any rate, I wish you luck on your "new" appointee. I respect your decision, even though I believe it is not the right one.

It's a small world in our profession, and we may again have reason to get together. I would look forward to it.

Best regards,

Turning Down a Job Candidate After He Was Assured He Was Hired on a Handshake Commitment.

Situation: A world-famous academic institution conducted a highly publicized search for dean of their school of business administration. You are a professor and head of the search committee for the nominating board. After interviewing many candidates, the committee zeroed in on a distinguished business professor at another well-regarded university.

You told him the position was his and that a contract was being drawn up. He went home with the belief that this was a done deal and so informed his family and several confidantes.

Then something happened. Another candidate, a newcomer to the selection process, came into view and swept the nominating board off its collective feet. He was their last-minute choice. By dint of personality and academic credentials, he is the individual they concluded they must have for this important post.

Now the news must be given to the person who was previously informed that he was selected. Concern must be shown for his sensitivity and reputation. But, however it is said or done, the university's reputation must not be blemished.

Strategy: Do not call him initially. First send a letter to his home. Then call him.

Let him down as gracefully as possible, extolling his credentials. Try to convince him that it is to his advantage not to take the post, which was a factor in the board's decision. Propose the thought of working together on future projects.

LETTER TO THE CANDIDATE

January 14, 1994

Clarence Van Clemens, Ph.D.
3 Apple Tree Lane
Ukiah, CA 41302

Dear Dr. Van Clemens:

You may at first consider this to be an unfortunate piece of news. But I'm sure that in the long run you will instead think of it as a fortuitous message. The board has decided to appoint another candidate to be dean of the Thorndike Business School. This came about after very painstaking deliberations.

Throughout all of our discussions, your name came up as being extraordinarily qualified, which is the reason we had so many sessions with you and invited you to meet with several of our faculty members.

However, we came to the conclusion that the academic philosophy you display at your present institution and in your writings would not blend with the direction we take here. We don't, by any means, disagree with your school of thought. It is just a difference of cultures, which would put you at a disadvantage.

This eleventh-hour decision took much soul-searching. We kept coming back to the point that you wouldn't care to adjust to the academic concepts at Thorndike. Nor would we expect you to do so. Your achievements are greatly admired by everyone here. You have our best wishes on your future endeavors.

By all means, let's stay in touch now that we've gotten to know each other so well. We hope you will give us the privilege of keeping you in mind for joint pursuits on projects that may come up in the future.

With kindest regards,

Clara Fine Kleinman

Clara Fine Kleinman, Ph.D.
Chairman, Search Committee

P.S.   We have set aside a budget, maximum of $5,000, to compensate you for any direct out-of-pocket expenses you incurred in the course of our discussions. We'll be happy to pay an itemized bill.

Letting Someone Down Easy When an Expected Promotion Didn't Come Through.

Situation: You are on the board of an investment brokerage firm. A department manager, who has been with you for many years, didn't get a coveted promotion. He thought he was in line for it, but the board decided he wasn't ready. It was felt he may have reached his zenith where he is. A young outsider was hired, which could worsen the slight.

    You don't want to lose him, and you don't want to shred his morale. He's very good at what he is doing, and it would be hard to replace him right now. Further, a disgruntled employee can be a problem.

Strategy: Send a personal letter to his home. Tell him he is so indispensable in his current slot that the board couldn't see their way clear to move him. It was a decision they made reluctantly because they knew it meant a lot to him. But his value to the business as a whole has to be uppermost. You want him to know he could be in line for good things in the future. Give him a raise.

LETTER TO THE PERSON'S HOME

January 24, 1994

Mr. Oscar Fite
421 Poplar Drive
_____

Dear Oscar:

The hardest thing in the world for me to do is to disappoint you on the investment director spot. You are just doing too good a job running the municipal department, and we can't spare you in this important position. The directors said it would be too difficult to get another person to fill your shoes.

We therefore tapped an outsider, Harry Bishop of Harper Securities, for director. Keep in mind, your job is just as important to the company as Harry's. The directors all agree with me on this. Your future here is better than ever. You can be assured that there will be other opportunities for promotion around here.

To convey our appreciation for the great job you've been doing, we are providing a salary increase to you. The amount will be shown in a separate note. In addition to putting more money into your bank account each month, I hope it will help assuage any letdown you may feel.

Keep up the good work, Oscar. You are an important part of the team.

My warmest regards to Phyllis.

Best wishes,

Lou

Mollify Your Friend's Disappointment. You Put Him in the Running for a Vendor Contract at Your Company. He Lost Out.

Situation: You are a sales manager at a proprietary drug manufacturer. A new merchandising program was developed, which required letters to be mailed weekly to a large number of doctors and pharmacists nationally.

Your friend is a principal at a direct mail company, and you invited him to go after this business. You know his work and that his company is well regarded. You would like him to have this assignment. You asked your colleagues to consider him.

He made an all-out presentation that ate up quite a bit of his company's money. It was competent and professional, but another company wound up with the business. You argued with your colleagues on your friend's behalf, but it did no good. The winner had previously done good work for the company. They had proven themselves.

Strategy: You told your friend on the phone, but you want to follow up with a letter to assuage his disappointment—and to recognize the solid effort he made.

You also want to mitigate your embarrassment and console your friend by assuring him a preferred hearing on the next piece of business that comes along. You don't want this incident to stand in the way of your relationship.

LETTER TO THE FRIEND

January 11, 1994

Larry O'Hara
President
Acura Mail Marketing

_____

_____

Dear Larry:

As in a ball game, one team wins, and the other loses. It was very close. It went into extra innings and, unfortunately, the other guy scored the winning run.

I want you to know that you had my support all the way, but I lost by one vote in a knockdown stormy session. What finally tilted the scale was that PNO had done business with us before and did a good job.

Larry, I know this doesn't do you any good now and that it's small consolation, but everyone here was impressed with your presentation. The amount of work and the smart thinking you put into it was obvious to us all. You did a great job of showing what you and your company can do.

That's why, in a way, you won—that is, if you want to consider the seeds you planted for the future. You are assured of a crack at other projects that come up. And when they do, you'll be in a preferred position because the people here now know you and like you. Sometimes it takes a couple of shots to hit the bull's-eye.

Warm regards,

A Job Recommendation for Someone You Fired. You Want to Help the Person Without Lying.

Situation: As director of lab research at a pharmaceutical company, you had to fire one of the research scientists. He was not entirely effective on his own, needing more supervision than his rank called for. He also botched up a research procedure. He's a nice guy, a willing worker, and likable. But in the final analysis, he didn't cut the mustard.

A prospective employer of this scientist asks you for a written evaluation.

Strategy: Be careful about what you say, as there could be repercussions. At the most, you should give a barely noticeable hint that your ex-researcher did not measure up under his own power and that he needed an undue amount of supervision. Besides, you want him to land a job.

April 14, 1993

C. Raj Hadeema, Ph.D.
Vice President, Director of Research
Caspar Pharmaceuticals, Inc.

_____

_____

Dear Dr. Hadeema:

You asked me for my evaluation of Dr. Wilson Rogers, which I am most pleased to provide you.

Wil was a fine presence in our diagnostic medicine lab as a senior research associate for the past five years. He is a learned scientist who works tirelessly and with great effort on his assigned projects. He adheres to established scientific principles.

I don't have to tell you that not all research leads to a commercial triumph, by any means. Most do not pan out or are marginally successful. Dr. Rogers was a member of the team that developed several successful formulations, but the endeavor he was put in charge of during the past eighteen months did not result in an acceptable product. Dr. Rogers performed to the best of his ability.

Because of a restructuring of priorities, we abandoned the research concept that Wil headed up. This concurred with a corporate staff reduction; thus, Dr. Rogers was not transferred to another division.

This, regrettably, caused Wil's departure. We wish him well.

Very truly yours,

Mary Wang

Mary Wang, Ph.D.
Vice President,
Director of Research

MW:jr

A Reference Letter for a Worker Who Was Fired for Out-and-Out Incompetence.

Situation: A production manager at a packaging company was fired after ten months on the job—for grossly unsatisfactory performance. You are the VP he reported to, and you are asked to send a written reference to a company considering him for a job. Basically, he was badly organized and a faulty production planner. He made some costly mistakes.

Strategy: Discretion is the watchword. There must be no damaging statements, even though he was fired for cause.

Have the letter come from the human resources department or a minor executive. Short, formal, safe, innocuous, without anything outwardly undermining his chance to be hired.

LET GO BECAUSE OF GROSS INCOMPETENCE

September 9, 1994

Ms. Agatha Enright
Vice President
Dual Delivery Systems, Inc.

_____

_____

Dear Ms. Enright:

This is in response to a letter you sent to Mr. Theodore Sherman requesting our evaluation of Jackson Miller, who worked here from August 9, 1993, to May 11, 1994.

Mr. Miller was generally liked as an individual by his fellow executives and other people who came in contact with him in the course of his activities here. He brought a pleasant and cordial atmosphere in his work area and he attended to his assignments with enthusiasm and a desire to do a good job.

It is difficult for me to provide further information about Mr. Miller, except that there were no specifically negative statements in his personnel record.

Very truly yours,

Leonore Malkowitz
Assistant Director,
Human Services

LM:jr

How to Fire Your Lawyer.

Two strategies:

I. Friendly.

II. Unfriendly.

Situation: You are the plaintiff in a lawsuit, seeking sizable damages. Your attorney told you that you have a good case. He assured you that the law was on your side.

It's now in the midst of discoveries, depositions, filings, and so on. You don't believe your lawyer is handling it well. He is giving you evasive answers or nonanswers to your questions. It's a reason to worry.

A friend recommended another lawyer, better suited for this kind of case and with an impressive track record. You met and liked him. You decided to switch.

Strategy I: You don't want to show your displeasure at the careless way your lawyer is handling your case. Tell him who is taking over, a big-time lawyer. Tell him, as well, that the new attorney will call on him for help, and you hope he'll be available. You had previously asked his opinion in an offhanded way on the feasibility of such a move, so it's not a complete surprise.

You don't want to cause any rancor. Alienating your former attorney may hurt you. You want to keep his goodwill.

FRIENDLY—YOU WANT TO RETAIN HIS GOODWILL

November 22, 1993

Mr. Jackson Schwardon
O'Hara, Schwardon & Harris

_____

_____

Re: *Perry vs. Doctrino*

Dear Jack:

I'm sure you'll agree with me on the move I'm now making in the case. After a lot of deliberation, I have decided that this suit should continue with another lead attorney. In fact, I touched on it with you a couple of times and got the notion that you were in agreement, which is why I'm doing this.

You have done a wonderful job in setting up the case so far. You've established a firm bedrock of documents. Now, for the next stage of litigation, I decided to engage Arnold Spiro of Spiro & Partners. I'm sure you know of him and that you'll agree with this choice. Please let me know if you have any misgivings.

I hope you will get involved when called upon. Arnold made it very clear he wants to be able to look to you for help.

Please be good enough to transfer all documents to Spiro & Partners within the next week. Mr. Spiro has a list of what to expect. Send me an up-to-date bill as of November 26, 1993. There are to be no charges after this date.

Jack, I want your talents to be on hand when any other legal problem arises. Let's talk further—I'll call you for lunch.

Best ever,

Joanna Perry

Joanna Perry

Strategy II: You don't have to be deferential or spare your lawyer's feelings. He's been sloppy on an important matter in your life that is causing loads of worry. You are bitter.

Professional ethics call for him to turn over all your records to your new attorney. You don't have qualms because the new lawyer will stay on top of the transfer. Besides, you have the originals of everything. Your ex-lawyer has copies.

November 22, 1993

Mr. Jackson Schwardon
O'Hara, Schwardon & Harris

_____

_____

Re: Perry vs. Doctrino

Dear Jack:

I came away from our meeting on Wednesday, March 14, dismayed at the inadequacy of your preparation in answering the latest series of inquiries. Very little has been done since my previous meeting with you on October 12.

In fact, I've been displeased all along with the way your firm is handling this case. My unhappiness has now turned to serious misgivings.

I have therefore engaged another law firm, Spiro & Partners, for this matter. Arnold Spiro has a list of all documents and will call you in a few days to arrange a transfer. He expects your cooperation, which I'm sure you will not withhold.

Send me a bill for all outstanding charges through November 26, 1993. There are to be no charges after this date.

I'm sorry I had to take this step, Jack.

Very truly yours,

Joanna Perry

Joanna Perry

Revive Your Chances for a Big Job. You Sense Your Interview Flopped.

Situation: You were interviewed for a top job at a high-powered financial services company. When you walked out you knew in your gut that it didn't click. The job is a big plum. You desperately want to redeem your chances.

Strategy: Send a letter to the person who led the interview. Give him a few relevant tidbits that you didn't say at your meeting, things that might put another perspective to your candidacy. It must be brief. Make a heroic effort. It's a bold shot, the odds may be against you, but it's certainly worth the effort.

LETTER TO THE PERSON WHO LED YOUR INTERVIEW

December 15, 1993

Maxwell Perez
Senior Vice President
Bulwark Investment Management, Inc.

_____

_____

Dear Mr. Perez:

Thank you so much for the opportunity to meet with you and your colleagues. There were a couple of questions you asked me that I then wasn't free to answer, since I had to make certain that I wouldn't divulge anything confidential.

After checking, I found that I am now able to give you the information you wanted.

> The Succulent Foods stock offering, which I shepherded along every inch of the way for my firm, amounted to $1.2 billion. It was successfully concluded in four weeks. This was a big coup for the firm, and I got a great deal of praise for it.

> I am assured I will be free to draw on my contacts in the financial community, which will make me a valuable asset in your New Offering Department and likely in other divisions as well.

Needless to say, I'll be delighted to provide other information you wish to know and that I'm free to disclose.

It was a real pleasure seeing you. Please think more about how I will fit in; I will, too. Regardless of what happens, we shouldn't let our relationship lapse. Let's get together soon. I'll call you.

Best regards,

Find Out Where You Stand on a Prospective Job Offer. You Counted on It. You Need It.

Situation: You are among the top ranks at an investment banking empire. Your major responsibility for the past five years was supervision of the various loan acquisition and funding activities of a worldwide conglomerate that specializes in communications equipment and software.

You developed a close relationship with the client-person you take orders from, the chief financial officer. You are buddies. Your strength with this account draws the resentment of your company's chairman and the chief executive officer, which predestines you for the trash heap at the opportune time. You know it, for sure.

Pow! The time arrived. Protocol at your company is to change the guard on a big account every five years so as to avoid any talk of possible ethical transgressions. It's usually adhered to. Your client couldn't save you because it's an established policy. You were even in the anomalous position of recommending your successor.

You are now without any duties, waiting for the cleaver to fall, hoping for a decent severance package. A year ago, you knew this would happen. Your ace in the hole is that your client told you he would give you a job when the time was ripe. The time is now very ripe.

Your ex-client is somewhat vague. He hasn't said no, but he hasn't said yes. You think it's in the works. Should you count on it? Two meetings were scheduled with him, but he called them off at the last minute. Your phone calls have not been returned lately.

Jobs are scarce, if available at all, at your level. Is something you counted on for the past year now a mirage? Your nerves are piano-wire tight.

Strategy: Send your client-friend a letter to his office. Mark the envelope: *Private. Open Personally, Please.*

Ask him not to keep you in the dark. You will soon be ousted from your office, and you need a job. Note that the height of your ambition is to work for your ex-client. You would like to know one way or another.

Tell him that whatever comes of it, your friendship remains intact.

LETTER TO THE EXECUTIVE YOU RELIED ON

September 9, 1993   Private—Open Personally, Please.

Mr. Richard Ebersol
Executive Vice President
Paragon Enterprises, Inc.

_____

_____

Dear Dick:

As you can imagine, I'm in an uncomfortable on-the-shelf position right now. There is no mention of having to leave Ingram's premises and payroll—so far anyway—but the day is clearly coming.

At any rate, I have to make a move. Hopefully, the right one.

We had been talking for some time about my coming aboard at Paragon. Personally, I would like nothing better than to work for you in my next and final career move.

I know you, I know the company, I know the people there. And you, above all, know me. After all, I've been working with your company for many years.

You are obviously extremely busy, especially now with your new acquisition, which is why it's been so hard to get to talk with you. I called a few times but you were tied up and haven't had a chance to get back.

I just wonder how it now stands. Should I consider myself slated for Paragon? If so, when do you think it will happen? Is it in the cards, but there's a temporary holdup? Is it doubtful? Is it something that's not now doable?

I'd appreciate hearing from you as soon as you have a few minutes. It would be good if we could get together for dinner to talk about this.

Whatever happens, Dick, it will certainly have nothing to do with our friendship.

Best regards,

A Career Wipeout. Outright Sexual Harassment.

An episode involving two people:

Letter A: Accuse your supervisor of sexual harassment.

Letter B: Supervisor retorts—defends his job, reputation, and future.

Letter C: Response to supervisor's retort—you deny his story.

Situation: You are a senior salesperson in ladies sportswear at a local branch of Harrison's, a large department store chain. You are a woman, thirty-three, ambitious, you've been there four years, and you were recently promoted from sales clerk.

Your department supervisor, a fiftyish married man and father of three, has been coming on to you the past four months, in private only, with no witnesses. He speaks to you with sexy innuendoes. He tells dirty jokes and uses obscene expressions to make a point. He touches you "accidentally."

There is the hint, spoken indirectly and innocently, that he likes your work and that you have the ability to advance if only you would loosen up. He says you are too aloof and too rigid in dealing with people.

He maintains a proper outward demeanor, which increases your frustration and misery. You repeatedly try to get your supervisor to stop, but he persists. Is this the way to get ahead in the company? You are in a trap.

Strategy: You can't let this frustrate your career goal. Why toss away four years of hard work and good future prospects? In time, perhaps you'll advance to buyer.

You send a confidential memo to the store manager, a man. Factual, unemotional. You note that you are trying to keep this private and within the store. You would be terribly embarrassed if it got out. You also want to protect the store's reputation.

The Denial:

The accused supervisor is confronted with the damaging memo and is asked for a written response. He categorically denies the accusation, betraying no sense of worry. This is unbelievable. He has an impeccable record at the store and has always conducted himself with rectitude. He has a fine future ahead of him.

And after all, he's been married for twenty-two years. He is a model husband with a loving wife and three children.

He doesn't go into detail at this point about the accuser and avoids personal criticism. He does not want to say too much. He remembers: Anything he says can be held against him.

Response to Denial:

As the victim and the accuser, you must respond to your harasser's denial. Why would you put your career, your reputation, and your whole future on the line? You still want to keep this within the company walls. You can get tough, but not now. Try hard to avoid a public furor, for it might backfire. Even if you win, you could lose.

COMPLAINT TO THE HEAD MANAGER ABOUT
THE HARASSER

October 14, 1993   Private and Confidential

To: Mr. Nikola Copernicos
         Vice President, Store Manager
         Harrison's

From: Fleur Delaura

It is with much pain that I must report an ongoing pattern of sexual harassment over the past four months by my department manager, Mr. Peter DeMentes. I very much wish to keep this a private matter.

Mr. DeMentes has been making subtle but explicit advances towards me through-out this four-month period. They are in the form of sexual innuendoes, dirty jokes, obscene remarks, and "accidentally" brushing against me. All this has taken place in his office or the stockroom when no one else is present.

I've been strongly discouraging these advances and making it abundantly clear that I find his actions reprehensible. Despite this, it persists.

Mr. DeMentes pointedly implied that my refusal to be "friendly," my "attitude," may be blocking my advancement in the company.

I prefer not to go into further detail in this letter. You can be sure I would not make this serious charge without justification. It was a painful decision to write this. I was agonized over it for a long time.

Thank you for giving this your attention. I leave it in your hands.

Respectfully yours,

Fleur Delaura

To: Mr. Nikola Copernicos
        Vice President, Store Manager
        Harrison's

From: Peter DeMentes

I categorically deny Miss Delaura's unsubstantiated and ridiculous charge. It is completely without foundation.

Frankly, this is a shocking surprise, for I regarded Miss Delaura as a good employee. All of my contacts with her were for business purposes only, and we have both maintained a strictly formal demeanor.

After all, Mr. Copernicos, I am a devoted family man. I have a loving wife, two daughters, and a son. I would not treat any woman in a way that I would not want someone to treat my wife and daughters.

I find the actions Miss Delaura describes as repugnant. It is inconceivable to connect this with me, especially considering my nature, my religious beliefs, my reputation, and my family values. The manner in which I have conducted myself in the store has always been at the highest level of executive rectitude.

It is for others to presume what caused Miss Delaura to make this charge. I am writing this letter with compassion in my heart for her.

Very truly yours,

Peter De Mentes

RESPONSE TO THE RETORT

October 21, 1993

To: Mr. Nikola Copernicos
        Vice President, Store Manager
        Harrison's

From: Fleur Delaura

The letter you showed me that Mr. DeMentes addressed to you was naturally no surprise.

I can only say that what I told you previously is the truth. I'm not a troublemaker. It hurts me greatly to bring harm to anybody.

Now I'm forced to bear the extra burden of having my rationality questioned. Everyone who has had any contact with me, in the store or elsewhere, will say this is absurd. My reputation, my uprightness, and my good sense speak for themselves.

I had my choice of keeping quiet, quitting my job, and going elsewhere. But I value my position at Harrison's. I don't want to throw away four years of conscientious effort, recently rewarded with a promotion, not to mention the prospect of a good career at this fine company. All I want is a fair chance to advance on my merits alone.

As I said before, I want to avoid any public exposure if at all possible. The turmoil and embarrassment that might come from the involvement of legal authorities would devastate me.

May I respectfully suggest that Mr. DeMentes be reprimanded and cautioned, which should obviate the need for carrying this matter further.

Sincerely,

Fleur Delaura

Subtle Sexual Harassment. Stop It.

Situation: You are a secretary in the purchasing office of a transportation company. You are twenty-three, outgoing, and ambitious. A coworker in his late thirties takes a fancy to you and constantly tries to engage you in cozy talk. His conversation when you are alone is peppered with off-color humor and suggestive remarks.

You are uncomfortable. You feel like a quarry standing alone out in the open.

He is careful. There is nothing explicitly indecent that you can pin on him, but his intention is clear. And it has to stop.

You spoke to him about it, judiciously so as not to put a big dent in his self-image, but he apparently didn't get it. You want to avoid any backlash against you.

Strategy: Put it to him in writing. A short letter, more chummy than hostile, explaining your discomfort and declaring without reservation that his innuendoes and overtures are unwelcome and must stop. You enjoy his company as a co-worker, and would like to be office friends. *That's all.*

You add that you don't want to cause any trouble, implying that you might have to take the next step if he continues.

IN-HOUSE LETTER TO THE HARASSER

November 9, 1993   **PRIVATE**

Jim Thornton
Supervisor, Purchasing Department
and Fellow Laborer

Dear Jim:

I know we get along well, and I like working with you. I also know you enjoy working with me. Shall I say a bit too much?

Being a proper young lady, I find that the way you talk to me at times, the way you get "friendly," is disturbing. It's not right, and it has to stop.

I see you as an attractive man, Jim, and you are a lot of fun. But I am definitely off-limits.

I hope you take this in the amiable spirit in which I intended. I don't want to have to make waves.

Your office buddy (that's all),

Lucille D'Amato

Lucille D'Amato

Discreet Racial Bias Is Holding You Down.

Situation: You are an African-American woman, a brand manager in a famous packaged-goods toiletries and cosmetics company. You are typecast, assigned ethnic products rather than big-volume, high-profile brands that can get you noticed—the brands that can send a career soaring.

You are well liked and admired for your bright, quick marketing sense and your keen intellect. There is no overt sign of racial bias. It is an attitude of your being apart, of having a "different" background. This abstract pall hangs over you and you have to fix the problem of being shunted away from the fast track.

Strategy: Send a memo to the top person in marketing in a sealed envelope marked private. Make no waves whatsoever. State that you believe there is no intentional prejudice, but you are being subtly yet strikingly thwarted from enhancing your career. All you want is a chance to prove your mettle in the corporate mainstream.

IN-HOUSE LETTER TO YOUR DEPARTMENT HEAD

March 10, 1994

To: Mr. Marcus Silverman
        Senior Vice President, Marketing
        Sanders & Pratt Products Company

From: Betty Ann Watson

Dear Mr. Silverman:

I had to muster up a lot of courage to send this memo. I trust it will have no adverse bearing on my status in the company.

As you know, I'm a product manager in the Beauty Products Division, having been here four years. I am the only African-American product manager in this division.

It seems I have a unique place here as a specialist for this ethnic market. The two brands that were developed for the black market were assigned to me. This has been a great experience, but it is now time for me to move on to an area where I am not typecast.

Please understand that this is not a racial issue. Indeed, I'm sure my supervisors have no bias whatsoever. I value their friendship and their counsel.

There just seems to be a condition where I am singled out as being a representative of the African-American community. The general understanding is that I know this consumer group better than anyone here and, therefore, that I am the logical manager to head up these ethnic brands.

My professor at Wharton, where I received my MBA, said this could happen. I didn't think it would happen here because of the company's reputation for fairness and tolerance, which is in no way the issue here. It's a matter of a glass ceiling that I have to penetrate.

I'm honored to be working at S&P. It is a wonderful career choice. May I please be judged on my ability, without any regard to ethnicity? All I want is the opportunity to advance on my merits in the corporate mainstream.

                        Respectfully,

                        Betty Ann Watson

Gender Bias . . . a Stop Sign on Your Career Path. Bypass It.

Situation: You've held mid-management positions at one of the world's outstanding hotel management companies for the past sixteen years with an impeccable record. You are one of the few female assistant managers at a major property. Despite an outstanding performance in these significant mid-management assignments, you haven't risen to become the general manager of a hotel.

Whispers have come through the grapevine that the chairman doesn't consider women to be appropriate hotel general-manager material. "Let's face it," he is reported to have said, "the top bosses at our hotels have to socialize and have a close rapport with the leading figures in their communities. They must have a cordial relationship with the corporate bigwigs, the politicians, the influentials, and they are mostly men. They have to drink with them, entertain them, amuse them, and a woman doesn't fit this role. Furthermore, a woman's child-care responsibilities have first call on her time and energy, and she can't give 100 percent to her job." This is the chairman's prevailing position.

You have reached your zenith, strapped and frustrated. This is not what you diligently trained and sacrificed for in academia and on the job.

Strategy: Send a letter to the executive VP, who handles operational matters, including personnel policies. He is also the chairman's top aide. He parrots the chairman's wishes, but can also advise him on what may be prudent and wise.

Bring ivory tower management up-to-date, into the modern world, and into acknowledging that superior job performance and management skills are gender-blind, even considering the taxing duties of the hospitality industry.

Realistically, you may not change the chairman's antiquated notions very much, but he has to be made to realize that he is way out of step with reality; that he is nurturing a fallacy, an unfounded, unacceptable bias that could hurt the business.

In terms of hardheaded practicality, you know that justice and the law, science, cold facts, and predominant public sentiment are on your side. The chairman and his aides are aware of it. You can be sure the executive you address will thoroughly check out your personnel record, which is very commendable.

You will likely give a nudge that puts your name up front for bigger things. You are a showcase candidate to shatter the glass ceiling of gender.

IN-HOUSE LETTER TO THE CHAIRMAN'S TOP AIDE

November 23, 1993

Mr. Ernest R. Sommers
Executive Vice President
Hospitality Management International, Inc.

_____

_____

Dear Mr. Sommers:

May I ask you to consider a matter of utmost concern to me and, I'm certain, to quite a number of other people in our company. In broader terms, I believe it is important to the long-range good fortunes of HMI. In essence, it will help maximize our profit-making potential by taking full advantage of all of the wonderful talent we have here. My personal situation will clarify the issue.

For the past four years I've served as the assistant manager in our Chicago property. Prior to this I held assistant manager posts in Costa Rica for three years, and in San Antonio for four years.

Before that I spent five years as an executive below the assistant manager level in San Juan. So you see, I've been with HMI for sixteen years—eleven years as an assistant manager, and currently at one of our choice properties. My personnel ratings have been in the top 10 percent wherever I served.

There appears to be a formidable barrier that is preventing me from being promoted to general manager. To my knowledge, no woman has ever been appointed general manager of an HMI property, or for that matter has attained any senior management post. I believe my academic training, experience, and performance equals or possibly exceeds several of my male colleagues who passed me by and rose to higher positions.

This frustrating situation understandably discourages me and, I assume, other women in this organization. There is untapped talent here, waiting for the opportunity to perform to full capability.

It gives me great pride to be a part of HMI. My uppermost ambition is to succeed in this company and to further contribute to its outstanding reputation in the hospitality industry. I am willing to be transferred to any location that offers greater rank and responsibilities. I am asking for the opportunity to show the full magnitude of my worth to HMI.

Most respectfully,

Dolores Fernandez

Dolores Fernandez

DF:jr

Your Company Is Leaving You Twisting, Twisting in the Wind.

Situation: You are a regional sales and marketing manager at a major airline. The FBI is probing around on a rumor of price-fixing with another large carrier. The finger is on you because you have occasionally been seen socializing with your counterpart at this competitor.

There is no hard evidence of any wrongdoing on your part. But your company is getting ready to make you the sacrificial lamb if something bad comes up so as to get it behind them with the least damage.

You will not be the patsy, and you don't want to hire a lawyer at this point. It would be very expensive and even possibly imply that the Justice Department is on the right track. A publicized allegation of wrongdoing can destroy your career, even if it is eventually found to have no merit.

Strategy: Write a letter to the senior VP of marketing, with a copy to the president, categorically stating your complete innocence. From where you stand, the feds will not be able to find any credible evidence of your complicity in anything like this. It's a fishing expedition, and you are unequivocally clean.

Your company must give you full support in dispensing with this. You will not be out front all alone.

LETTER TO YOUR SUPERVISOR, COPY TO THE CEO

December 6, 1993

Mr. Peter G. Travis
Senior Vice President, Marketing
Worldwide Airlines, Inc.

_____

_____

Dear Mr. Travis:

I want to briefly review here the situation of the FBI poking around to check on the possibility of a price-fixing scheme with Ajax Airlines. Charges were apparently made by what we are led to understand is an anonymous source, likely a vindictive competitor. Rumors are rife, and it is far from pleasant.

I'm in the middle. Along with Ben Thompson at Ajax Airlines, I'm one of the so-called suspected culprits, but not because they found anything on me. It's because I head the department that supposedly conspired with Ajax.

Mr. Travis, I categorically deny that I ever engaged in any price-fixing plot, with Ajax or anyone else. As for Ben Thompson, if he did it with anyone, it was not with me. Nor did I ever violate any law or regulation or any company policy or rule.

If Worldwide had similar pricing as another airline, it was never planned in advance. You're well aware, Mr. Travis, that we constantly monitor what our competition is doing, as they do us. You emphasized many times that we have to match or be below our competitors' fares on similar routes. That's how we survive as well as we do.

Ben Thompson and I are acquaintances. We sometimes lunch together and we socialize occasionally, but I assiduously avoid giving him any inside information whatsoever. I follow this same policy with anyone outside this company. To my knowledge, no one in my department leaked information about pending fares.

I expect Worldwide to stand fast and fully support me in this inquiry, whether it involves the Justice Department, the FAA, Congress, or anyone else. I am perfectly clean. My reputation, my future employment and advancement, and the well-being of my family must not in any way be compromised.

I don't see how anything can come of this except, unfortunately, some groundless publicity. Naturally, you can count on me to elaborate on the statements I've made here with government authorities or anyone else. Based on what I now know, I will defend the company with a clear conscience.

Truly yours,
Lawrence DeAngelo
Western Regional Manager,
Sales & Marketing

Copy: Mr. F. Scott Curtis,
        President & CEO

You Got Turned Down for a Highly Publicized Top Job. Explain It to Your Peers.

Situation: A financial colossus was looking to fill a top spot. It was well publicized. You, a senior-level investment manager at another well-known firm, were named in the press as one of the four candidates on the short list.

You didn't get the job—a highly visible turndown, embarrassing and demeaning. You are concerned that you may now be considered to be glued to your level, not equipped for an upward leap as an out-front policymaker.

Strategy: You have to recoup your dignity with your peers in the industry. Send them each a letter to spread a favorable story for public consumption. You didn't want the job and actually turned it down. Be gracious and statesmanlike.

LETTER TO YOUR PEERS

October 31, 1993

Mr. Larry Burton
President
Bulwark Assets Corporation

—————————————
—————————————

Dear Larry:

You must have read in the papers that I was on the short list for the CFO's slot at Dexter Securities. Mary Roth took the job, and I wish her well. To my mind it's good for both Dexter and Mary.

I think you'll be interested in knowing the inside story of why I didn't take it, without my revealing any privileged information.

Jerry Noodleman, the board member who headed the search committee, got in touch with me through a headhunter. I didn't want to pursue it and said so. Why should someone start something like this when he is happy where he is, especially at a place like Ashton, Crawford? I'm getting what I want and doing what I want—what anyone could want, really. I am told the sky's the limit for me here.

The headhunter said he just wanted my advice and asked if he could set up a meeting with Noodleman. Naturally, I told Cap here what was happening, and he said, "See them, but be careful. Don't let them talk you into anything that's not right."

Noodleman introduced me to George MacTavish, the chairman, and some of the other board members, and we chatted about what the job required and who would be good for it. Ostensibly this was the reason they wanted to see me. I mentioned a few names.

Afterwards they asked me to consider the job, but I took Cap's advice. Even if Cap hadn't said anything, I wouldn't have been interested for good reasons, such as those I mentioned before as well as others that I'm not free to talk about. It has nothing to do with Dexter as a company or the people I saw. It's a wonderful company and a great bunch of people.

I thought you'd want to know what really went on, what with all the rumors bouncing around and the reports in the press.

Call me when you get into town and we'll break bread. Give my best to Edith.

Warm regards,

Money Matters

A Good Customer Wants to Drastically Cut Your Bill.

Two letters: long and short form.

Situation: You are the chairman of an industrial engineering company that designs and produces manufacturing tools and machinery. The president of a valuable client wants to deep-cut a bill that was mutually agreed to in writing. His staff told him that the job, though well done, was completed in far less time than was anticipated. He sent you a letter stating this. They have muscle because they are a good source of future income.

If need be, you are willing to reduce the bill somewhat to preserve the amicable bond you have developed—but not by the amount the client noted. You want to get as much money as possible without compromising the relationship and, at the same time, solidify the goodwill of this client.

Answer the client's letter with your letter, asking for a meeting to settle the matter. It's important to talk face-to-face, top executive to top executive. The issue and the money involved are important, and it can only be resolved at the top.

The letter is to show a sincere willingness to cooperate. It's been a rewarding relationship, and as always you want to act in the client's interest.

At the same time, you want to invoke the client's sense of fairness and understanding when he learns the facts. The meeting will clarify these facts. His staff probably gave him half-truths so as to be heroes by saving a lot of money.

Two letters are shown. One expresses your goodwill and desire to cooperate and includes some of the key details that buttress your case. This way, the client knows the guts of the issue prior to your meeting.

The other is a short form, not giving any details but expressing a strong desire to be cooperative. And it notes that the client will be fair and understanding when he's apprised of the facts. In this version, you want to conserve all your ammunition for the personal meeting.

Both letters proclaim your willingness to bend over backwards to do what's good for your client.

LONG FORM, GIVING DETAILS

April 19, 1994

Mr. Timothy Georgeson
President
Communications Specialties, Inc.

_____

_____

Dear Tim:

This is to respond to the points raised in your letter of April 15. I am doing this in the spirit of working for the benefit of CSI. Throughout our relationship, your interests have been of primary importance to us. As such, we will be guided by your budget constraints and will give you our best possible cooperation.

Please consider my position, Tim. When you know all the facts, I'm sure you'll look at this with your usual sense of fairness. Below are the issues that I want to clarify.

Although your R&D staff came to us with the Telesphere specifications and product archetype, we had to start from scratch to develop the manufacturing process. This entailed a great deal of original thinking, much research on tool design, and countless episodes of trial and error. Not to mention frequent eighteen-hour days and weekends.

The result was a practical way of getting your product to market at a competitive cost and at a normal profit margin for CSI.

We came through for you before, and this time we did it again—successfully and within your time frame. But now your people say that the time we devoted to this job was less than is warranted by the fee—and that the fee should be cut in half!

Tim, bear in mind that the $300,000 fee was a fixed amount for this assignment, mutually agreed upon. The fact that we completed the job faster than anticipated attests to our engineering skills, originality, efficiency, and experience in tackling this kind of problem. Also, as noted before, we put a vast amount of overtime into it.

Should we be penalized for knowledge, efficiency, and devotion to the task you gave us? If it took longer than anticipated, would we have asked for more money? Of course not.

The important thing is that the assignment was accomplished successfully, meeting all specifications with total satisfaction on the part of your staff.

Let's have a meeting to discuss this. I'm confident we can resolve it in a way that is right for both of us.

Best regards,

SHORT FORM, NO DETAILS

April 19, 1994

Mr. Timothy Georgeson
President
Communications Specialties, Inc.

Dear Tim:

You raised certain points in your letter of April 15, and I'd like to have the opportunity to review them with you. It has to do with our agreed-upon fee for designing the Telesphere manufacturing process.

Please understand that this is in the spirit of working for the benefit of CSI. We will be guided by your budget constraints and are prepared to give you the most cooperation possible.

Tim, when you know all the facts, I'm sure you'll look at this with your usual sense of fairness. Let's have a meeting and we'll be able to resolve it in a way that is right for both of us.

Best regards,

A Good Client Is "Slow Pay," but You Can't Afford to Alienate Them.

Situation: You are a sales VP at a telemarketing company. One of your accounts is a heavyweight magazine publisher who is responsible for about 30 percent of your income.

Unfortunately, they have a nagging flaw. They are slow-pay on your company's invoices—sixty to ninety days. You are told to get them to a thirty-day cycle because a lot of money is involved each month, which causes a heap of problems.

The last thing you want to do is rock the boat with this account, but you are compelled to follow orders and straighten out their lackadaisical way of paying bills.

Strategy: Send this client an almost apologetic letter pointing out the problem. Ask for their solicitude. Make it seem like you didn't want to bring it up, but you were pushed to the wall by your company's comptroller. This hard-nosed bean counter is the heavy—it's not your doing.

LETTER TO THE CLIENT'S TREASURER

April 7, 1994
Mr. Dennis O'Toole, Treasurer
Acme Publishers, Inc.

_____

_____

Dear Dennis:

I had a hell of a hard time writing this letter. I had refused to do it because I felt it was out of order. But our comptroller and head bean counter, Joe Spurno, put my feet to the fire. I'm sure when you read this, you won't see a problem, but I nevertheless feel lousy sending it.

It seems that our bills get paid in sixty to ninety days or more at times, which has become the pattern. This is a long time for us, because it means putting out a lot of money over two to three months to service your business. For example, at this point you are $185,000 past due sixty days or more. As the schedule now stands, it could be as much as $250,000 by next month.

You see, we are obliged to pay our suppliers' bills in thirty to forty-five days, and our internal expense outlays, which are basically salaries and office overhead, have to be current.

Although I realize you generally pay your vendors on a normal sixty-day cycle, which sometimes stretches to ninety days, could you please see your way clear to push payments through to us in thirty days, which may at times overlap to forty-five days?

Even though our company has the resources and creditworthiness to back up these finances for you when necessary, it comes to big numbers on a continuing basis, which makes a problem for Joe.

I don't have to elaborate on what a marvelous relationship we have and that we've been doing inspired work for Acme. I'm sure you're aware of it. It makes me feel so good to know that our work has generated profits for you during the entire time we've been privileged to handle your account.

Please understand Joe's position—and again, take note, if you will, of my personal aversion to writing this letter. Please let me know if there's a problem.

Sincerely,

Frank Hooper

Frank Hooper
Vice President

A Client Isn't Paying Your Bills. Lots of Money Is Way Past Due.

Two letters:

I. Request they pay past due bills and stay current.

II. If they don't comply, resign the account.

Situation: You are a senior executive at an ad agency, overseeing a major electronics client. The people are charming to work for, but with one defect. They are slow payers—often agonizingly slow—past due many months. You hate to dump them and sue, because they represent good income and you know they are far from broke. The money is good, eventually. But you can't afford to bankroll them.

   At any rate, if you sue, there will be legal costs. And it will take months, maybe years to get your money—perhaps not all of it.

   You don't want to blow this account, and you don't want to say anything that will diminish your chances of getting them current.

Strategy: *Letter I:*

Write a firm letter, but as pleasant as possible under the circumstances. You can't go on this way and must stop your services until they are current. But you emphasize that you want to continue if at all possible. Register the point that your work has been excellent and that there's no reason to hold up payments.

Letter II:

Time passed and they didn't pay up. You now send a letter resigning the account. Next step: Sue them. You have no choice.

REQUEST THEY PAY PAST-DUE BILLS AND
STAY CURRENT

April 13, 1994   By Registered Mail

Break-A-Way Electronics Inc.

_____

_____

Attn: Mr. C. David Benson
        Executive Vice President, Marketing

cc: Mr. Angelo Fortunato, President
        Ms. Elizabeth Doherty, CFO
        Mr. Gerald Martin, Comptroller

Dear Dave:

I was given strict orders to write this letter.

It has to do with your overdue bills, going back as far as eight months. A schedule is enclosed.

It amounts to $658,000 past due, of which $212,000 is delinquent six months or longer. Much of this is out-of-pocket expenses, which we have paid. And we're currently working on assignments that call for additional expenditures.

All of these bills were well documented and approved by you and your staff. Your people are happy with our work, which is still in use. Our previous requests for payments were acknowledged, but nothing of substance has been received.

Our finance department told our account group to discontinue all work on your account until you become current. It stands to reason, we can't continue as bankers for Break-A-Way. Quite frankly, it's beyond comprehension that a company of such distinction as Break-A-Way could be so unmindful of their financial obligations. Our comptroller said he needs an answer within the next four weeks.

I hope you understand that we are taking this action with much regret. We have no choice. Our people have been knocking themselves out on your account and the work is exceptional, as you have remarked many times.

Dave, sending this is painful to me personally, and I hope we will be able to continue working together. We are so well experienced in your business, and we have so many new ideas to help keep Break-A-Way growing. We feel we can still have a wonderful future together.

Truly yours,

Bill Kayson

Bill Kayson
Senior Vice President

RESIGN THE ACCOUNT BECAUSE THEY HAVEN'T PAID

May 13, 1994   By Registered Mail

Mr. C. David Benson
Executive Vice President, Marketing
Break-A-Way Electronics, Inc.

_____

_____

cc: Mr. Angelo Fortunato, President
       Ms. Elizabeth Doherty, CFO
       Mr. Gerald Martin, Comptroller

We have not received a satisfactory response to the issues raised in our letter of April 13 regarding delinquent bills. We are therefore obliged to resign your account, effective June 10, 1994. Your payments are due for all unpaid invoices and for all work in progress as of this date.

Upon receipt of your payment in full we will transfer all artwork, materials, and copy files.

We're doing this with much sorrow. We all liked working with you and are proud of the results you've been getting. We've been very effective for Break-A-Way.

I'll be pleased to have our paths cross again under better circumstances.

Regretfully,

Bill Kayson

Bill Kayson
Senior Vice President

Break Through Bureaucratic Stalling and Go to the Top to Get the Money Owed You.

Situation: You are the owner of a wholesale stationery company, and you purchased some office equipment on a bank credit card. The merchandise was stolen. The bank is obliged to cancel the charge in accordance with a special promotion to card customers that they've been advertising for months.

You are getting stalled by the bank's middle management. You called and wrote the marketing director, but there is still no action.

Strategy: Write a letter to the marketing director again, but this time make sure copies also go to the bank's top brass. Technically, you are not bypassing the director, but he knows you are letting his boss of bosses know of his intransigence. It also serves notice of the obligation of the bank's top management.

You want to show your know-how and determination by citing the government agencies that have jurisdiction in these matters. If you complain to them, the bank may well have a problem, with their management bearing responsibility. This will shake up the bank and get you action.

Send it by certified (or registered) mail, return receipt, for greater impact.

The copies to the bigwigs should be addressed to each of them personally in separate envelopes, but not certified or registered.

LETTER TO THE MARKETING DIRECTOR, COPIES TO THE CHAIRMAN AND CORPORATE COUNSEL

January 19, 1994   By Certified Mail

Mr. Barry T. Joonow
Vice President, Director of Credit Card Marketing
Assured Bank

_____

_____

Mr. Louis Lewin, Chairman & CEO
Ms. Rona T. Mapery, Sr. VP & General Counsel

On September 21, 1992, I wrote to you about $3,497.10 Assured Bank owes us because office items purchased on my credit card had been stolen. Your advertising states that you will cancel a card charge if such a situation occurs.

I spoke to your customer service representative about this, and at her request I mailed a copy of the sales slip and a statement of what happened, together with a police report.

To date, I have not received this refund on my credit card account. When I called your office, I was told it was being reviewed and that there may be a question as to the validity of my claim.

I then wrote to you on the above date, and so far you have not responded. Nor have I been able to get through to you personally by phone. I have already paid for phone calls and correspondence, not to mention the time I spent on this.

I can't believe that Assured Bank would engage in misleading advertising.

Mr. Joonow, if this is not resolved within the next thirty days—that is, by February 22, 1994—I will be obliged to contact the State Banking Department, the Attorney General's office, and the FTC to obtain what is rightfully owed me.

Very truly yours,

Samuel Herbert, President

Enclosures with supporting documents.

A Careless Goof by a Financial Manager Cost You Money.

Situation: You informed the investment broker that had handled your bond fund that you have selected another money management house. You instructed them to make the transfer. However, they transferred it to the wrong money management company, a firm you didn't even know. It took three weeks for it to be straightened out—and only after you made a lot of noise. Your fund was in limbo all this time.

It couldn't be traded or sold, and you lost money because the price fell day by day and you weren't able to sell. This is a clear case of broker incompetence and carelessness, perhaps because of pique at losing this business.

Strategy: Send a registered letter to the president of the company that goofed. Give him the facts and state you want to be paid the money lost, which your accountant and financial manager are determining. This alerts him to start on his own financial analysis.

Give him ten days to respond following your statement of loss, after which you'll seek restitution through the proper authorities.

LETTER TO THE BROKERAGE HOUSE CEO

February 22, 1994   By Registered Mail

Mr. T. Roger Quinn
President & C.E.O.
Shelby, Leonard Investment Brokers

_____

_____

Dear Mr. Quinn:

Enough! This comedy of errors has got to stop.

This has cost me money. Plus insufferable anxiety and an inordinate amount of time trying to get it straightened out.

Here is the situation:

Shelby has managed my fund since February 1987. On January 27, 1994, at 2:00 P.M. I specified that it be transferred to Washburn Bank & Trust. This was confirmed in writing the same day.

By mistake, the fund was transferred to the Parleau Fund. The reason for choosing Parleau is convoluted, and I will not discuss it here. Suffice it to say, it was an inexcusable blunder.

This fiasco was not discovered until seven days later when I inquired of Washburn why they hadn't received my bond holdings.

Shelby kept dodging the problem, saying Parleau should make the correction. Parleau threw it back to Shelby, and so on.

I prevailed upon Washburn to act as referee and to effectuate the transfer, which they are doing. I now think my fund is finally where I want it to be.

The issue is not cleared up by any means. During the three weeks my bond fund was in limbo, the price started to go down. I wasn't able to sell while watching the price fall to my dismay and financial loss.

I don't have to remind you of your responsibility in this. My investment manager and my accountant are now ascertaining the amount of Shelby's liability, which will be forthcoming in the next few days.

Needless to say, I have complete documentation for all the statements mentioned here.

Very truly yours,
Elizabeth Pryor Gibson

P.S.   If I don't hear from you within ten days after I send you the financial report of my loss, I will be obliged to seek redress through official means.

A Bank Is Trying to Squirm Out of a Mortgage Commitment on Your Office Condo. It's Favorable to You, but Not to Them.

Situation: The bank accepted your application for refinancing a second mortgage on your new office condo at a very good rate, which they were promoting at the time. Since then, the rates have gone up.

   The bank keeps losing your application. They stall, they misplace your documents, and then they put you off. With gnashing teeth, you are determinedly trying to inch the process forward.

   Finally, the bank acknowledges the application. But they impose an impossible condition, not brought up before, that will effectively kill the deal. Thus, they won't have to live with the low rate.

   If you start all over at this or any other bank, it will be at a higher rate.

Strategy: Write a certified letter to the VP in charge of the mortgage department. Make it factual and restrained. Point out the problem and indicate the bank's obligation to honor their commitment.

   You wish to maintain pleasant relations with the bank, so it's best to avoid a nasty or threatening demeanor. On the other hand, you are determined to pressure the bank to honor this mortgage loan.

LETTER TO THE VICE PRESIDENT IN THE MORTGAGE-LENDING DEPARTMENT

January 20, 1994   By Certified Mail

Ms. Regina Harper Greene
Vice President, Mortgage Lending
Upstream National Bank, International, Inc.

_____

_____

Dear Ms. Greene:

We're sorry to have to call on you for help. But it's come to the point where it is important for you to clear up a predicament we're having with your department; specifically, that your department is not fulfilling the bank's legal obligation on our application to refinance the second mortgage on our office condo in Franklin Park, Illinois. What follows is a summary of the circumstances.

> Our application (No. 30217) was filed on August 17, 1993. We locked in the special rate you offered at the time and paid a fee of $450, which the bank is still holding.

> Every time we called to expedite this, a new person was in charge. We successively dealt with five different people. Each one said you had no record of the filing and asked us to fax the documents. So far we've faxed this material five times. Whenever we tried to talk to an individual, we were put through an obstacle course. The bank records are obviously disorganized. Finally, we got approval. But it was subject to a new condition that wasn't in effect or even discussed or hinted at when we filed. It is an impossible condition. Anyone could be led to believe the bank imposed it in order to renege on the refinancing deal.

> The new condition is that the condo committee has to give up the right of refusal to the resale of this property. In other words, in the case of foreclosure the bank can sell it to whomever they choose, at whatever price they choose.

> There is no way the condo committee would ever agree to this. It is contrary to their charter, contrary to their rights, and contrary to any normal condo conditions.

The rates have gone up since the filing at Upstream and other banks. It would be burdensome for us to refinance at the present rate.

We cannot tolerate the egregious condition the bank imposed on this loan, done summarily and after the fact. We are fixed on the rate that the bank advertised and agreed to under the conditions that were in effect at the time. The bank accepted our application in good faith, and we don't believe you can walk away from it.

Thank you for your time in reviewing this. We're sure you will see to it that Upstream honors its commitment.

Very truly yours,

P.S.   We have long been Upstream customers. The bank holds the first mortgage on this office complex and has serviced us on a number of other loans. We have enjoyed our relationship, and we would like to continue doing business with Upstream.

Your Bill to a Customer Is More Than the Contract Called For. Explain It.

Situation: As the owner of a printing company, you finally got a chance to bid on a big job for a new customer. They contract out a lot of printing, and you have been courting them for a long time.

   The specifications are tough as to quality and deadline. You lowball your bid so as to be sure you get the assignment, hoping for the best.

   Three quarters of the way to completion, you find you can't finish the work for nearly what you quoted. It would mean a sizable loss, which you can't afford to absorb even if you wanted to. You have to ask for more money.

Strategy: Write a letter explaining the higher charge. It must be plausible, so that the price will be acceptable without much protest.

   Your contention is that the customer is to blame. They made changes beyond anything that could be reasonably anticipated, and you want to make an on-time delivery without sacrificing quality. Tell them that you are eating a big part of the additional cost.

   Furthermore, point out that the printed piece will be superb—work that they will be proud to show, within their organization and outside. You will make them look good. Isn't this what's most important when all is said and done?

LETTER TO THE CUSTOMER

March 3, 1994

Mr. Herbert H. Rothman
Vice President, Credit Card Marketing
2nd National Bank

_____

_____

Dear Herb:

It took a lot of doing, but we made the recent changes on the mechanicals that you and Tim ordered, and we're on track in getting the work done on time. This caused a lot of extra expense because the visuals and some of the type had to be completely redone.

We probably could have squeezed through without making all this extra effort, but it wouldn't have come out right. That is, it wouldn't have been perfect. You said you wanted perfection, and that's what you're getting. No compromises, no kidding.

Your staff had previously asked for other changes that turned out to be time-consuming. Frankly, we put a lot of overtime into your job to meet your due date and specs. We did not want to let you down on quality or timing.

All of these production changes have added 19 percent to the cost over what is shown in the production order. It went from $50,000 to $59,500.

We're able to bring it in at this price because we're eating a big part of the overtime cost. In addition, our paper supplier raised the price of the stock after we gave you the quote, and we're not charging you for this additional cost. If we charged you for all the extras, the price would be over $68,000.

As it stands, you are getting a terrific bargain. But more importantly, you are getting wonderful paper stock and the highest-quality printing. You will have flyers you will be proud to show your chairman and president. A beautiful piece like this is sure to increase your consumer response—the extra expense will more than pay for itself.

Thanks so much, Herb, for the opportunity to serve you.

Best regards,

P.S.   Let's have lunch or dinner next week. I'll call your secretary for a convenient date.

Dunning a Close Friend for a Business Loan Owed You.

Situation: You came through for someone close to you when he needed money for his business. It was three years ago, and he had been courting you at the time. The relationship cooled, but the tender feeling didn't. You are still good friends.

It was not a small sum. He asked for $60,000, which you lent him. All you got back was $30,000, which was a year and a half ago. He seems to be taking advantage of the relationship and hasn't made a move to pay back the rest.

Too much time has passed without bringing it up. And you are now in urgent need of the money for your business. His business is doing fine, and he can afford to pay up.

Strategy: Send a chummy letter with affectionate undertones. The debt won't stand in the way of friendship, but there is a pointed reminder that the money is due and that you need it. Make a veiled reference that legal persuasion would work but is not necessarily on your mind. That is, not yet.

LETTER TO THE FRIEND

April 16, 1993

Mr. Harry Camanakis, President
Desiree Beauty Care

_____

_____

Good morning, Harry,

It's come to pass. . . . I have to quote James Baldwin, the author:

"Money . . . is exactly like sex, you think of nothing else if you don't have it, and think of other things if you do."

You thought of money (not sex) three years ago because you needed it (the money). Now I'm thinking about money for the same reason.

In other words, I need the rest of the money I lent you—$30,000 plus $1,500 interest, a total of $31,500. I still have your loan note.

I understand your business has been quite good and that you should be able to pay, so this is not an unrealistic request. (Among friends we don't use the awful word demand.)

Harry, I don't want to have to make a legal case out of this because your friendship is so important to me. If need be, you can pay me $10,000 now and $7,000 a month for two months, with $7,500 in the third month. Naturally, it would be great if you rob a bank and pay the whole thing at once. I'll be in touch with you next week to see which of these options is best for you.

Honest, Harry, if I didn't need the money for my business, I wouldn't press you. But I do and I must. That's how important it is.

Thanks so much, Harry. I know you'll complete your obligation as you had promised. We'll always be friends.

With much affection and
admiration,

A Law Firm Upped Their Bill Mightily, Way over Their Advance Estimate.

Situation: The bill came in much higher than they indicated it would. More time was charged, and more copies of documents had to be made, creating additional charges that hadn't been specified in advance.

Professionals sometimes eat up more time than expected when they get into a project, and they are extremely reluctant to agree to a cap. At $200 to $300 an hour, it mounts up quickly to big numbers when the meter starts to run.

Strategy: Caution: Be nice. Try to avoid getting rough with a lawyer. Remember: It costs them hardly anything to sue you, but it costs you a bundle to defend it. Ask to settle for the original estimate because you can't afford to pay the extra amount. Note that you will need more legal help in the future, at which time more money will be available. Good luck.

LETTER TO THE PARTNER WHO HANDLED YOUR MATTER

April 15, 1994

Mr. Oliver T. Golden
Darwin, Golden, & Meister
Counselors-at-Law

—————————————

—————————————

Dear Mr. Golden:

Thank you for the information you provided and for your advice. This will help in formulating our immediate decision, although we will need more legal assistance when we get to the next stage in this new business venture.

We decided to take this piecemeal approach in seeking legal guidance because we don't want to go beyond a $10,000 charge at this time, which is the outside limit of what you said it would be. That's why we were surprised and shocked when we received your bill for $16,440. It is much more than we are in a position to pay at this early stage.

Your bill noted, among other things, extra research costs over what we had discussed in order to have auxiliary backup. You didn't tell us you were going ahead on this, and, truly, we didn't think we needed this extra assurance for our current purposes. If you had asked us in advance, we would have told you not to go over the $10,000 charge.

Mr. Golden, we value your expertise and legal judgment, and we certainly want to continue with your firm as this project grows to what will be considered a major enterprise. But for the present, we ask your cooperation in keeping our bill at $10,000, which had been agreed to, and which, as I mentioned before, is the absolute limit of what we are able to pay now. It goes without saying, our legal budget will be higher in our next stage.

Thank you so much for your consideration.

Cordially,

You Were Floored by the Bill a Law Firm Sent. There Was No Advance Estimate.

They were hell-bent on legal maneuvers and piled up heavy fees:

Letter to the attorney.

Letter to the other defendants in the case.

Situation: You were employed by an engineering company and left for another job at a company in the same industry. Six fellow employees at the same level also switched to various competitors—all of these job changes taking place within a six-month period. You all have stock options in your former company.

Your former company instituted a blanket suit, naming the seven of you as codefendants. The purpose of the suit is to recover your stock options at no cost because of what they consider to be a legitimate loophole in the issuing document. They cited collusion in that all of you left within a short time. There was no collusion—it was coincidental.

They also charge that you use your ex-company's privileged information at your new locations, and you all have to answer the charges.

The seven of you banded together and hired a law firm for a common defense. You had given the firm's partner on your case a retainer and asked her to let you know of impending expenses before she proceeded to pile them up at the rate of $200 to $300 per hour plus expenses. She went to work on the legal chores without providing an estimate of expenses, as you had requested.

Without warning, she sent each of you a bill for $6,500 covering the first four weeks, with a description of the legal work that was done. She also sent an agreement form to sign, authorizing her to continue her work and be able to bill for it on an ongoing basis.

Strategy: Draft a letter to the attorney that expresses your feelings and documents your request for the information you want—a detailed accounting of ongoing expenses and an agreeable cap.

Send a copy of this to the other defendants along with a letter to them, to relate your displeasure about the lawyer's conduct and to show your attitude on legal expenses—as well as to arrive at a common understanding on how to proceed.

LETTER TO THE ATTORNEY ON THE CASE

December 10, 1993

Ms. Sara Sobolev
Connors, Melnik Law Firm

_____

_____

Re: Your Letter and Bill of November 3, 1993.
     Casuist Production Engineering Ltd.

Dear Ms. Sobolev:

Your letter and accompanying bill came as a distinct surprise—and an unnerving jolt.

   A. First of all, we had agreed that you are to let me know in advance of any activity you would undertake that would result in a major expense. I consider this amount a major expense.

   B. There is no indication as to how long this case will take and the amount of legal effort and bills. Signing your fee agreement on a going-forward basis amounts to a blank check.

I'm sure it is not your intention to seek sanction to move ahead without some kind of cap or protection device to guard against outlandish payments in terms of what the case is worth. It may get to the point where it doesn't make sense to proceed.

   C. I am asking for an opinion from you as to the worthiness of our case, how much is at stake, and what our chances are.

I know you can't predict what a judge and jury will do, but you do know, from your experience and knowledge, the strength of our legal position, the odds of the plaintiff winning, and the advisability of making a countersuit. In other words, is it worthwhile to pursue this at the level at which you are proceeding?

Please let me know so I can decide how I want to proceed.

Respectfully,

Cynthia Fuller

Cynthia Fuller

LETTER TO THE CODEFENDANTS

December 10, 1993

To the Parties Defending the Lawsuit of Casuist Production Engineering Ltd.

Janice Bomar	Linda Sue Hager
Paul Caplitsky	Perry Mitchell
Drew Reynolds	Paula Herbert

Dear Friends:

This is about the letter from our common law firm, Connors, Melnik, which I assume you received. I was nonplussed—shall I say shocked?—by the size of their bill, which came without warning, and also by their request for an open-fee agreement on ongoing activities. It amounts to signing a blank check, which, frankly, is against my nature. I'm sure you feel the same way.

I'm enclosing a copy of the letter I am about to send to C.M. I'd like to get your opinions. Did I reflect your attitudes? What do you think about this whole matter? Do you have any other questions that should be put to C.M.?

I think we should have a meeting of the minds as to what we want to do and how much money we should put towards it. I also think we have to marshal our forces to rein in C.M. without impairing our position.

Let's get together or have a phone conference.

Warm regards to all,

You Are Being Mistakenly Billed. It Continues Uncorrected.

Situation: You returned office supplies that were bought through a catalog. The catalog company didn't record the return and keeps sending you bills, with interest added every month because the bills are in the past-due format on their computer.

You phoned and were asked to send a letter with a copy of your return receipt. You did, twice. Later phone calls produced pleasant replies, apologies, and assurances that it was being fixed. The bill continues to come in every month, and the interest keeps piling up.

Strategy: Write a letter to the sales manager expressing your annoyance. Report the facts. Avoid invective or insults, but do let her know that you will charge for your time and expenses if this dialogue continues. It's a good way to get you out from under their pile of correspondence and stir up some action.

LETTER TO THE BILLING COMPANY'S DIVISION MANAGER

December 6, 1993

Ms. Sheila Hammerman
Catalog Manager
Newman's Office Supplies, Inc.

_____

_____

Dear Ms. Hammerman:

It's been said that patience is a virtue.

Does running out of it mean not being virtuous?

My patience and perseverance are being tested by Newman's Office Supplies. I am now calling on you to finally put an end to it. I'm sure it can be done very easily now that it's in your hands.

On January 10, we placed an order for equipment, chairs, and supplies amounting to $2,878.41, billed to our account. Part of the order totaling $1,260.08 was returned because it was not the color ordered. I have the return receipt for this. No replacement was requested.

Then it started. I've been getting a bill for the original sum every month for the past four months, which includes a 1½ percent monthly interest charge.

I called and wrote several times. Each time I get a prompt letter in response, but these are stock letters taken off the shelf. Your people just fill in the blanks. Newman's, it seems, has a generic letter to fit every possible contingency.

We don't have the advantage of stock letters. I have to compose a new letter every time I write. I and my associates have already spent much too much time writing and phoning. Ms. Hammerman, you must put an end to this.

This is to serve notice that if it is necessary for us to do anything more on this matter, we will bill Newman's for time and expenses, as follows:

Composing letters: $50 per hour
Typing and phone calls: $10 per hour
Postage, stationery, phone charges: To be billed at cost

My previous activities on this matter, including this letter, will not be billed, since I had not informed you in advance of my rates.

Thank you, Ms. Hammerman, I anticipate your prompt attention to this.

Very truly yours,
Mrs. Rebecca Sloane
President
Hudson Real Estate Brokers

Unaffordable Extra Charges on Repairs and Equipment.

Two situations:

I. No written confirmation of cost overrun.

II. Written confirmation of the extra cost.

Situation I: A contractor bumped up his bill for shelving, rigging, and office furniture because of modifications he did not anticipate. The issue of extra charges was specified on the phone but not confirmed in writing. The price hike was considerably more than was verbally cited—a real shocker.

Strategy I: Send the contractor a letter noting your surprise and chagrin, and say you can't afford the cost overrun. Tell him that if need be he will have to take back the furniture and equipment.

Offer to settle. The contractor has little leverage. Removing the merchandise, particularly the shelving and rigging, would be costly, and besides, it was modified for your premises. He may not accept your first offer, but you'll probably be able to settle for less than the total overrun that was billed.

Note that you want to do business in the future, but from now on every cost must be specified in advance in writing.

Situation II: A contractor increased his bill above the original estimate, an overage that was confirmed was exceeded. The additional cost is a distinct financial burden.

Strategy II: You offer to pay the original estimated amount at once, with the additional sum to be paid three to four months later.

You want to avoid their having to go the legal route to get the full payment. You simply need more time to pay it all off.

NO WRITTEN CONFIRMATION OF COST OVERRUN

January 25, 1994

Super D Office Equipment Service

_____

_____

Attn: Ms. Edwina Sherman, Vice President, Sales

Dear Ms. Sherman:

I say this with agitation as well as concern. When your bill came in (No. 11030, copy attached), it floored us. Literally.

The shelving, rigging, and furniture was originally priced at $138,275, which was confirmed by our purchase order. We grant that you had to make modifications on the merchandise, which you told us about. However, you didn't specify the full amount of the cost overrun. We had no idea the extra charge would be $33,050, which brought your bill total to $171,325.

Regretfully, we are not in a position to pay this additional money. Further, we believe the modifications are in large part your responsibility, since you did not have merchandise that fit our space needs, and you agreed to alter what you had in stock.

It is your option to take back the merchandise, which understandably would be costly for you and inconvenient for both of us. We certainly don't look on this with any favor.

We are willing to settle the bill for $15,000 over the original quote, for a total of $153,275. There is really no way we are able to go above this figure.

Since we both want to resolve this quickly, we ask that you let us know your position in writing at your earliest convenience.

Please, next time we do business together, let's pin all charges and extras down on paper before they take place. *Everything,* so there are no surprises. You have a good shop and good people, and we would be pleased to have you supply our needs in the future.

Sincerely,

WRITTEN CONFIRMATION OF THE EXTRA COST

January 25, 1993

X3 Computer Resource Ltd.

_____

_____

Attn: Accounts Receivable
        Oscar Steuben

Re: Your Invoice
        No. 34772

Dear Mr. Steuben:

We received the software we had ordered, together with your bill for new peripherals. The total is $22,370, of which the peripherals portion is $20,000.

We value this equipment, and your people did a fine job of installing and testing. Our monitors are working satisfactorily and up to expectations. However, your original estimate was $14,000, which we set aside for payment. We acknowledge that we later authorized additional components at the extra cost.

The cold fact remains, however, that we are not prepared to pay the additional $8,370 at this particular time. We are confronted with a tax surcharge that hadn't been predicted, and which has to be paid at once.

Please bear with us. We will be able to comfortably pay you the $8,370 difference in the next 90 to 120 days. Then we also want to talk about additional equipment to take care of expanded business volume.

We value your service and want to maintain a good relationship. Be assured, this bill will be paid in full.

Very truly,

Recently Purchased Office Equipment Is Unsatisfactory. You Want to Exchange It. Paid by Credit Card.

Two strategies, two letters:

I. Paid by credit card and the charge went through.

II. The credit card charge did not go through.

Situation I: An air-conditioner unit you recently bought from an appliance retailer for your conference room doesn't have enough cooling capacity. The salesperson had mistakenly told you it would be adequate. You want it removed and a more powerful unit installed. You paid by credit card.

Strategy I: The credit card charge went through. They have your money. You must invoke their goodwill to have them make the exchange. It's good to mention that the manager of the bank that issued your card is your ally. A retailer wants to have a good image with a credit card bank, particularly one in his area.
  Send a letter by certified mail, return receipt.

Situation II: You were able to cancel the credit card charge with the issuing bank before the payment went through. In effect, the supplier hasn't been paid.

Strategy II: You are virtually in control. Ask for an exchange. It's not a bad idea to bring in the name of the credit card bank manager for extra leverage.
  Send a letter by certified mail, return receipt.

CREDIT CARD CHARGE WENT THROUGH

January 13, 1994   BY CERTIFIED MAIL

Perfect Appliances And Electronics, Inc.

_____

_____

Attn: Ms. Irene Wentzel, Vice President and Store Manager

Dear Ms. Wentzel:

I'm sure you will understand our consternation and frustration when you read this. From the glowing comments we heard about your company, I am equally sure you will set it right.

It regards an Upstart 190 room air conditioner that we purchased for our conference room on December 21, 1993 (#134702, delivered and installed December 23). This machine doesn't cool sufficiently, even though your salesperson told us it has adequate BTU capacity for our room size of 22 feet by 35 feet.

The room temperature does not go below 78 degrees on a hot day, which is certainly uncomfortable. It goes without saying that we would have ordered a more powerful unit if there was any indication it was required.

Our credit card charge of $1,286.17 with Carol National Bank has gone through. But the manager at our branch told us they had processed many transactions from Perfect Appliances, and that there hadn't been any problems, and that we shouldn't be concerned because of your fine reputation in this community. She was certain you would replace this machine with one of greater cooling capacity. We are asking this of you at this time.

Ms. Wentzel, we're sorry for any inconvenience this is causing you. But it's good to know you will rectify the situation. You will have a delighted customer who will join our bank manager and other businesspeople in this community in vouching for your reliability.

Thanks so much. I'll talk to you soon about making the exchange.

                                        Best regards,

YOU CANCELED THE CHARGE BEFORE IT
WENT THROUGH

January 13, 1994   BY CERTIFIED MAIL

Perfect Appliances And Electronics, Inc.

_____

_____

Attn: Ms. Irene Wentzel, Vice President and Store Manager

Dear Ms. Wentzel:

I'm sure you will understand my agitation about the Upstart 190 room air conditioner we purchased from you on December 21, 1993 (#134702, delivered and installed 12/23/93).

It doesn't cool the room satisfactorily, even though your salesperson stated the BTU units were sufficient for the room size of 22 feet by 35 feet.

I have therefore asked my credit card bank to cancel your charge of $1,286.17 for this product and installation.

I would be very happy if you removed this appliance and installed another air conditioner with greater cooling capacity and, perhaps, a different brand, which we can discuss. The manager of the bank branch that issued my card said she has many transactions with your store without any problems, so I'm confident you will make good on this.

I'm sorry for the extra work this has caused you, but it's good that the situation can be rectified, and you will have a happy customer who will be coming into your store for many more purchases.

Thank you so much.

                                        Sincerely yours,

A Company Wants to Pay You, but Your Check Is Trapped in Its Data File. Extricate It.

Situation: You were laid off (i.e., fired), and several thousand dollars are owed you for severance and vacation pay—actually, over $30,000. The amount is beyond question and is not challenged. Nevertheless, it is trapped in a bureaucratic maze. You cannot decipher or even understand the problem when it's explained to you.

Time drags, bills are due, and you need the money. You can't afford to start a lawsuit. The company can easily afford to defend it, and a legal fracas would drag on and on.

Strategy: Send a letter to the company chairman. Say that if you don't get your money shortly, which is a cut-and-dried expense on their part and is not in contention, you will have to unwillingly put the proper government agencies on it. Appeal to his sense of compassion. You are a poor lone person versus a rich giant. This letter will be a good document if and when you seek legal help.

LETTER TO THE CHAIRMAN

September 10, 1993   By Certified Mail

Mr. David H. Solomon
President and C.E.O.
Manor Hotel Supply

_____

_____

Re: My letters and documents forwarded 7/1, 7/13, 8/17

Dear Mr. Solomon:

The whole issue boils down to this:

> When I was dismissed on July 29, 1993, the company owed me
> $30,628.00 in severance and vacation pay and unreimbursed expenses.

> I should add that this experience caused me to have anxiety and depres-
> sion, resulting in physical suffering, which a doctor can verify.

This approved amount that is due me has been confirmed by several of your
departments, including legal and accounting. But everyone I called has no inkling
of where the matter stands.

My intuition says this is mired in your accounting files or in your computer memory. My common sense says if I don't get a positive notification of payment by
September 30, I will have to reluctantly start the legal machine rolling with the
appropriate government agencies.

Why not be fair to an ex-employee and pay what you unquestionably owe? I'm
looking for a job and need the money. My paycheck has stopped, but my bills
haven't. Unemployment insurance hardly covers it. Please, Mr. Solomon, don't
keep me needlessly waiting any longer.

                                      Very truly yours,

Protect Your Broker Commission When There Is No Written Agreement.

Situation: A company in another state wants your printing company to produce their brochures. You find you can't handle it with your equipment and are subcontracting the job to another printer—that is, a third party.

    The third party asked you to sign an agreement guaranteeing payment. In effect, you would be guaranteeing your customer's payment. You don't want to take this risk.

Strategy: Two letters:

Notification to your client.

Notify the third party supplier.

Send the guarantee statement to your customer. He now knows you are using an outside supplier and who it is. You previously asked for a broker's commission on this job, and he approved with a verbal agreement. However, he could now deal with the third party directly and squeeze you out, neatly avoiding your commission.

If you ask your customer to sign a broker's agreement now, he might stall or refuse, which could sanction his not paying. Therefore, send him a letter confirming your verbal agreement. It gives you some protection, which is better than none.

At the same time, let the third party know in writing that you have a right to the broker's commission, which he may have to pay by increasing his bill to include it.

You've done what you can. It sounds convoluted, but this paper trail is the way to go in this situation.

This exercise is not nearly as good as a written agreement prior to starting the work, but it provides a basis for getting tough if you don't get paid. Anyway, it's worth the effort.

TO YOUR CLIENT

April 8, 1994   By Certified Mail

Victor Stepanian, Senior VP
Coup Promotions, Inc.

_____

_____

Dear Victor:

As we agreed, I got an outside source to produce the 500,000 printed flyers you need for your client's promotion. We weren't able to adhere to your specs for the precise die cut with our equipment.

Anytime Graphics is doing the job. I understand that you have previously done business with them directly. You should understand that I negotiated with Anytime to bring their price down $10 per 1,000 from their quote—from $35 to $25 per 1,000. This took a lot of negotiating, particularly in view of your tight schedule. You had originally said you were in a position to pay as much as $35.

Anytime wants a signed commitment guaranteeing the price and payment terms, which I'm not in a position to give. I'm enclosing it for you to sign and forward to Anytime, with a copy to me.

As the broker on this deal, my commission is a flat $5 per 1,000 pieces, which is what we agreed to. It is to be paid to me at the same time you send payment to Anytime. This comes to $2,500 for this 500,000 print run, and $5 per 1,000 for later print production with Anytime or any other printer.

I will handle the set-up details with Anytime and will keep this job moving.

We're delighted to be serving you, and I'm looking ahead to a boom promotion.

                                               Truly yours,

TO A THIRD-PARTY SUPPLIER WHO IS INVOLVED

April 8, 1994

Mr. Ferde Carew, President
Anytime Graphics, Inc.

_____

_____

Dear Ferde:

I sent your agreement to my client, Coup Promotions, for signature, since it is not in my province to assume this obligation for them.

I realize you had done business with Coup directly, but I am the broker in this project and am to receive a flat commission fee of $5 per 1,000 pieces for this 500,000 run and all subsequent runs.

As it stands now, I'm to get this payment from Coup. But this could change, and I'll advise you whether to add the $5 to your bill and send me the commission.

Truly yours,

Staying in the Best of Graces with Your Ex-Employer. A Lot of Money Is at Stake.

Situation: You just left a giant media conglomerate for a top spot at a competitor. A BIG going-away severance payment is due you—on paper. Your ex-employer, the company president, got his back up about your departure and threatens not to pay you. "Sue me," he says.

Strategy: It would be dumb to burn your bridges. It's smart to keep up a friendly connection with the head honcho of the company you left. Why squander a deep-rooted relationship? You never know when the connection can pay off, only that it probably will. Show him your admiration. All executives love flattery, regardless of how they may toss it aside.

Send a letter of regret that you'll miss his guidance, his counsel, and his company. Indicate that staying close will pay off for both of you. There's a small circle of top players in this industry, and your paths are sure to cross. You'll be making deals together.

The issue of the severance package is left unsaid. But it's in the wind, and this letter is intended to quell resistance.

LETTER TO THE EX-EMPLOYER

January 18, 1994

Mr. Donald T. Degraw
President
Data Connection Corporation

_____

_____

Dear Don:

As I look out from my office window here in the suburbs, what do you think is on my mind?

It's how I liked working with you, which I'll really miss.

Mostly, it was the valuable guidance you gave me. It was great tossing around ideas with you. I admire how you seized on strategies to make the business thrive, how we made competition sit up and take notice, and how we made decisions on the run. I don't think I'll ever forget the drag-out sessions we had in your office. But we sure got things done.

The lessons I learned—shall I say the training I got?—at DCC no doubt got me ready for the big challenges I have here. There's so much to do to grow this business and they gave me much leeway to do it.

The new technology that will soon be available to consumers will be mind-boggling. No one company can avail themselves of all of it. Part of my mission here is to set up partnerships, joint ventures, and parallel marketing for exciting new consumer services—entertainment, shopping, politics, investments, and personal counseling. You name it.

I'm sure we will be able to work and invest jointly, get a big jump on the industry, and make a lot of money together. We often talked about it. Don, that's the future, and it's coming up fast. In fact, it's here, staring us in the face. I can see our working together in the future. I'd like nothing better, because I know what you can do.

Give my love to Theresa. Jackie sends warm regards to both of you.

Have a great day,

You Can't Make Bank Payments That Are Due on a Business Loan.

Situation: You are the owner of a temporary worker franchise. Your company is financially strapped and can't continue making installment payments on a $100,000 bank loan. It's a three-year loan, and half of the payments have been made.

   You need more time to straighten things out. You may be able to resume payments in six months or so.

Strategy: Be candid and sincere in your desire to make good on your debt and maintain your reputation. It's caused by a temporary setback. Your condition looks viable and you should soon be in a position to pay. You need time.

   You want to appear intelligent, responsible, and worthy of confidence and trust. You value the relationship with the bank and with the executive you're addressing, and you'll be doing business with them for a long time.

   You will be liable for interest being accrued during the hiatus, which will increase your total interest on the loan. But you need a break for now on monthly payments for principal and interest.

   The underlying factor: Actually, the bank has little choice but to grant a hiatus, as long as they believe you are sincere and good for the money.

LETTER TO THE LOAN OFFICER VICE PRESIDENT

March 15, 1994

Mr. Roger McDevitt, Vice President
Standard Bank and Trust

_____

_____

Dear Mr. McDevitt:

May I prevail upon you for help in a special situation? It's about our installment loan for $100,000 (#82351), which calls for thirty-six monthly payments and on which we've been making payments for the past eighteen months.

As you know, we have been punctual in our payments to date, as with all our other financial responsibilities. We very much value our reputation and credit standing. However, a problem has arisen at this time.

We're undergoing unexpected expenses for emergency office repairs. In addition, there has been unusual difficulty in collecting a substantial payment from one of our customers. This customer has had a business setback that will soon be alleviated, and they have assured us of payment shortly.

This is a temporary condition caused by these two one-time occurrences. Our business is viable, which is certainly a good record considering the state of the economy. We've cut expenses to maintain an ongoing profit situation while still adhering to our normally high standards of customer service.

Mr. McDevitt, may we request that you suspend our loan payments for the next six months? We will then resume on schedule. As you know, we have been customers of Standard Bank and Trust for the past four years, and we expect to continue to be customers for many more years. We've had a pleasant relationship with you personally as well as a fine business relationship with the bank. We value both of these greatly.

Thank you so much for your cooperation.

Sincerely yours,

Jack O'Doul, President

JO:xx

Your Company Was Shortchanged on an Insurance Claim.

Situation: There was storm damage to your commercial building and adjoining parking lot. The insurance adjuster put your loss at $238,000. Your actual cost of repairs is an additional $53,000 after your deductible.

Strategy: Point out the error in a registered (or certified) letter, return receipt, to the head of claims at the company, and c.c. your broker. Attach a complete list of damages and the cost of each item of repair and compare it with the amount the company allowed. You already spoke to your broker, and it is agreed that you will write to the company directly.

Be amicable and assume they made an honest mistake. They are invited to come back and reassess the damage, although, understandably, repairs are in progress.

This is a lot of money. You have to be prepared to pursue this if they don't make good. Enclose the facts and figures with the letter. However, write with the assurance that the issue is cut-and-dried and that the company will pay the extra money.

LETTER TO THE INSURANCE COMPANY

September 27, 1993   BY REGISTERED LETTER

Mr. Roger Andrews
Vice President
Angelou Insurance Corp.

_____

_____

cc: Amalgamated Insurance Brokers

Re: Claim No. 30542
       32 Westminster Drive

Dear Mr. Andrews:

This is to report a sizable miscalculation in the adjustment of damages to my building and adjoining parking lot at the above address resulting from Hurricane Andrew.

Your adjuster estimated $238,000. The repairs are now being done and it's clear that the cost will be $291,000—$63,000 more than what your company allowed. With my $10,000 deductible, the amount of underpayment is $53,000. A full itemization and particulars are enclosed herewith.

Mr. Andrews, I want to stress that these repairs are necessary to bring my property to the state it was in before the storm. It is not to make any improvements beyond that condition.

I realize your adjuster was extraordinarily busy at the time and may have been hasty in his examination. I'm sure that Angelou Insurance will rectify his miscalculation.

As you can imagine, this has been a terrible experience for me and my employees. It's so good to know we have placed our trust in a fine, ethical company such as Angelou.

Thank you for your time in taking care of this matter.

Truly yours,

A Stockbroker Touted a Bad Investment. You Want the Money You Lost.

Situation: Your stockbroker talked you into an initial public offering. He strongly suggested it would be a good money-maker, a seldom-seen opportunity.

You are normally prudent with your hard-earned money, but you saw this as good advice from a supposed friend.

Eleven months passed, and you now have a loss of $32,400 on a $100,000 investment, which was still sliding southward when you were able to sell it.

You are distressed; it's making you physically ill; and you feel stupid about being conned. You desperately want to get your money back.

Appealing to the NASD, SEC, and attorney general will take months of delays and mounds of paperwork. It's questionable if they would see this as an important enough matter on which to launch their big guns. You have to prove duplicity or fraud. Consulting a lawyer is costly. Undoubtedly, other people have also been stung by this culprit. Could you start a class-action suit? If yes, how?

Strategy: Send the head of the brokerage firm a registered letter, return receipt, declaring your grievance. You tell him that his company's agent gave you a glowing verbal report, making statements that were not shown in the prospectus. You note that the company, in effect, knowingly allowed you to obtain misleading information. Include all the particulars.

The letter shows your awareness of the government authorities and industry bodies that monitor such matters but that you prefer not to have to involve them *at this time*.

Brokerage houses and other companies that handle money and are subject to official regulations are especially concerned about claims of misfeasance or unethical practices. They don't like to be investigated by the authorities. You have a legitimate beef that the company will probably check out thoroughly. Your loss may not be big enough in their eyes to warrant a fracas, and they may want to settle this and get it out of the way.

However, the company's attorneys may consider that a payment to you could cause legal problems, such as opening up a can of worms regarding their other investors in this and other offerings.

If a great deal of money is involved, or the company doesn't want to make good or has disappeared, government authorities and the courts may be the only option. You'll need a lawyer to represent you, a means of redress that is not the province of this book.

LETTER TO THE BROKERAGE HOUSE CHAIRMAN

November 17, 1993   By Registered Mail

Mr. Bailey C. Dickinson
Chairman and CEO
Dickinson, Stanley, Mathews, and Co.
Investment Counselors and Brokers

_____

_____

Dear Mr. Dickinson:

I am bringing to your attention a serious wrongdoing by an agent in your Detroit office, Mr. Oliver Buckley. It has caused me a large financial loss and much personal anguish, which has affected my health.

Mr. Buckley was very aggressive in selling me 1,000 shares of the initial public offering of LEX Biotech, on January 7, 1993, for $100,000. He spoke glowingly of the company's future. He said it was a vanguard entry in a zooming market, that it was doing cutting-edge research, and that new-product breakthroughs were in the pipeline.

I am very conservative in these matters, but I trusted Mr. Buckley. He was eloquent in elaborating the merits of this offering. Mr. Buckley caused me to believe I would make a profit of 20 percent to 30 percent on my investment within twelve months.

Instead, LEX, as you know, plummeted in value, causing me a loss of $32,400 when I finally sold the stock on November 8, 1993, to avoid further loss.

I realize there is risk in stock transactions, but this was a case of your agent pushing a very questionable investment with falsely optimistic information. It may well be that other people have similarly suffered severe losses as a result of this deception.

I did not contact the SEC, the attorney general, the NASD, or the N.Y. Stock Exchange Ethics Committee. I prefer to deal directly with you, Mr. Dickinson, as the chief executive officer of a well-known and reputable investment company. I demand that your company redress this egregious and unethical manipulation of my hard-earned money by putting $32,400 into my account. I will then consider it a closed matter.

If I do not hear from you by November 29, which is two weeks from the above date, I will be obliged to take further action.

Very truly yours,

Send Me Your Problems . . .

You are invited to mail the author a *workplace* problem on which you seek advice for a strategy that will help you compose a successful written communication. Your letter must have your correct name and address in order to be considered, which, needless to say, will be held in confidence.

I can't promise you a personal response, since a great many letters are coming in and each one deserves individual attention. I'll certainly attempt to respond to all proper and sincere requests.

There is the possibility that your problem situation, and the advice you get, may be incorporated in a book, magazine article, newspaper column, or other media venue, unless you specify otherwise. In such case, a pseudonym or initials will be used in place of your name and the organization involved for reasons of privacy.

Please mail your letter to the address below, and kindly include a self-addressed, stamped envelope.

Bernard Heller
P.O. Box 231069
Great Neck, NY 11024

I hope I can help you resolve your problem.

Bernard Heller

Index

About the Author

The author brings the experience and expertise of four decades as a hired practitioner of top-gun written communications—presentations, reports, documents, letters, memos—any and all devices in which pen is put to paper and fingers stroke a keyboard.

These communications were written on demand at the behest of companies, ad agencies, marketing firms, and nonprofit organizations to various publics, boards, departments, bureaus, institutions, and executive task forces. They enabled clients to make fortunes and enhance authority, respect, and power—or avoid the loss of same or even to avoid disaster.

Bernard Heller spent twenty years working for advertising agencies under some of the all-time toughest and ablest icons in the art of commercial communications. He rose through the ranks to the top management echelons on the strength of his communications and business building talents.

Mr. Heller then stepped out on his own, counseling clients in communications and sales. He was called upon to create business presentations, letters, reports, scripts, documents, and other written media in which ideas are invoked. He was also commissioned to develop new marketing opportunities via advertising, direct marketing, and other sales methods.

In the course of his business career, Bernard Heller worked with a great many companies and institutions of many sizes and in many fields—global behemoths, midsize companies, professional and industrial associations, and small enterprises. He dealt intimately with scores of executives at all levels—industrial titans, entrepreneurs, upper and midlevel executives, and rising stars.

Mr. Heller got a B.A. from Brooklyn College and later put in three years at Columbia University Graduate School.

Following college, Heller served four years in the U.S. Navy as a fighter pilot aboard aircraft carriers. This experience bred a deep respect for disciplined training and constant preparation in order to intuitively exert caution and calm efficiency in facing life-and-death situations. It brought to the fore the credo that the ordinary is routine, the extraordinary is the test.